Enhancing and Expanding Gifted Programs

The Levels of Service Approach

Enhancing and Expanding Gifted Programs

The Levels of Service Approach

Donald J. Treffinger
Grover C. Young
Carole A. Nassab
Carol V. Wittig

Prufrock Press Inc. • Waco, TX

Center for Creative Learning, Inc.
P.O. Box 14100–NE Plaza
Sarasota, FL 34278-4100
Phone: (941) 342-9928
Fax: (941) 342-0064
E-mail: cclofc@gte.net
www.creativelearning.com

Prufrock Press, Inc.
P.O. Box 8813
Waco, TX 76714-8813
Phone: (800) 998-2208
Fax: (800) 240-0333
www.prufrock.com

Contents

Figures

Chapter 1
Introduction

"Use what talents you possess; the woods would be silent
if no birds sang their song except those that sang best."
—*Henry Van Dyke*

The most significant message of gifted education is that we need to empower and enable students to develop and use the talents they possess. Our greatest opportunities, and our most complex challenges as well, are really about programming, rather than definitions or identification procedures or instruments. Through our combined years of experience in the field, spanning more than two decades, we have come to the conclusion that effective, quality programming is the very heart of gifted education. This book presents our approach to programming for talent development, in what we describe as the "Levels of Service" (or simply "LoS") approach. By service, we mean any activities, actions, or experiences that educators, parents, community members, or students themselves choose, construct, and carry out for educational purposes.

In our work, we use the phrases "talent development" and "programming for talent development" as efficient ways of summarizing the full message we hope the phrases will convey: "all of the efforts made—at home, in a classroom, in a school, in a school district, and in a community—to recognize, nurture, and celebrate the many and varied strengths, talents, and sustained interests of all students." Talent development involves a commitment and a challenge to create, differentiate, and carry out many opportunities to nurture students' strengths, talents, sustained interests, and best potentials.

This challenge addresses the need to provide effective educational opportunities for students who already demonstrate outstanding ability or accomplishments in many talent areas. These are the students whose needs are the focus of many gifted education initiatives in our schools. Our challenge also includes deliberate efforts to discover and develop the strengths and talents of many other students whose potential is often hidden or overlooked. These are students who, for a variety of reasons, are not involved in gifted programs. Finally, recognizing the power of the school, the home, and the community, the challenge extends to a new and even more inclusive opportunity: for educators, parents, and many community members to work in partnership, as illustrated in Figure 1.

Home

- Read! Read! Read!
- Manage TV wisely (less is better)
- Offer encouragement, express appreciation
- Provide access to and support for out-of-school activities, programs, and mentors
- Monitor homework
- Go on "field trips" together
- Apply constructive discipline
- Hold high standards, expectations
- Listen, be caring, and look for strengths, talents, interests
- Model and share your talents, interests

The Individual Student

School

- Offer appropriate, rich, varied, challenging curricula and instruction
- Hold high standards and expectations
- Use authentic assessment and learning (focusing on using or applying information)
- Create opportunities for talents and interests to emerge and be recognized, to develop, and to be celebrated

Community

- Places: zoo, museum, science center, college or university …
- Events: concerts, plays, exhibits, stories, fairs …
- People: community resource programs, mentorships …
- Groups: scouting, civic, religious, Junior Achievement …
- Programs: after school, weekend, summer courses, camps, institutes …

Figure 1: The "Ecosystem" of Talent Development

By working in partnership, parents, schools, and communities can create programming that will "bring out the best in every student." (Figure 2 presents, in a lighthearted way, an illustration of the risks of trying to do the job alone.)

You Can't Do It Alone

A letter from an insurance company asked a policyholder to clarify the reason for a claim related to an injury on the job. The insured individual replied as follows:

Dear Sirs:

I am writing in response to your request for more information regarding Block Six on the Insurance claim form, which says "Cause of Injury." I put there, "trying to do the job alone." Here is your additional information.

I am a bricklayer by trade. On the day of the injury, I was working alone, laying brick around the top of a four-story building. I finished and had about 500 pounds of bricks left over. Rather than carry them down by hand, I decided to put them into a barrel and then lower them by a pulley that was fastened to the top of the building.

I secured the end of the rope at ground level and went back up to the top of the building. I then loaded the bricks into the barrel and swung the barrel out with the bricks in it. Then I went down and untied the rope, while holding it securely to assure the slow descent of the barrel.

As you will note in Block Four of the claim form, I weigh 145 pounds. Due to my shock at being jerked off the ground so swiftly, I lost my presence of mind and forgot to let go of the rope. Between the second and third floors, I met the barrel coming down. That accounts for the bruises and lacerations on the upper part of the body. Regaining my presence of mind, I held tightly to the rope and proceeded up the side of the building until my right hand jammed into the pulley. This accounts for the broken thumb.

Despite the pain, I kept my head and started to clamber onto the roof. At approximately the same time, the barrel of bricks hit the ground, and the impact knocked the bottom out of the barrel. Devoid of the weight of the bricks, the barrel now weighed about 35 pounds. I again refer you to Block Four of the claim form, and my weight of 145 pounds. As you would guess, I began a rapid descent.

In the vicinity of the second floor, I met the barrel coming up. This explains the entries about injuries to my legs and to the lower part of my body.

Slowed only slightly, I continued my descent, landing on the pile of bricks left by the bottomless barrel. Fortunately, only my back was sprained and the internal injuries were minimal. I am sorry to report, however, that at this point I lost my presence of mind and let go of the rope. And, as you can imagine, the empty barrel crashed down upon me.

I trust this serves as clarification of what I meant by stating that the accident was caused by trying to do the job alone. Please know that I am *through* with that approach!

Figure 2: The Risks of "Doing the Job Alone"

At every level of the LoS approach, we consider many and varied places, resources, and settings. People, places, and resources outside the school contribute to high-quality instruction for all students in many ways, providing "springboards" for more extensive talent development opportunities and experiences. The contributions of home and community support, extend, expand, and enhance (rather than supplant) the school's activities and services. Schools and teachers cannot do the job alone; moreover, educators must not use outside factors as an excuse for refusing or failing to accept the challenge of talent development ("We don't have to be concerned with talents of that kind … the students who are interested can have those experiences elsewhere."). Within the school, various professionals may also share the responsibilities for recognizing and nurturing students' strengths and talents. In the LoS approach, programming for talent development is not just what "the gifted teacher does" for the students "in his or her program." Nor do we propose that the classroom teacher should have sole responsibility; no one person can be "everything for everyone." In the LoS approach, we emphasize the importance of a productive, collaborative relationship among classroom teachers and professionals with specific training and experience in talent development. We often refer to these specialized professionals as LoS Catalysts. In practice, schools have described them as talent development teachers, talent coordinators, or gifted programming specialists, and you will encounter all of these terms in the stories and examples in this book (since we used the titles that were actually used in the real setting). Figure 3 summarizes some of the important dimensions of the partnership between the classroom teacher and the LoS Specialist.

A Professional Partnership for Talent Development

Classroom Teacher	LoS Catalyst
1. Being a talent spotter; search actively for all students' strengths, talents, and sustained interests.	1. Facilitating planning at school and district level.
2. Teaching with multiple groupings and varied activities and assignments.	2. Initiating, coordinating, and supporting many services (LoS I & II).
3. Providing time and support for student-initiated projects.	3. Leading, networking, and supporting plans and services (LoS III & IV).
4. Engaging students in productive thinking.	4. Facilitating contacts and connections with outside resources.
5. Designing and using authentic learning experiences or activities.	5. Serving in liaison role (staff, students, parents, administration, and the community).
6. Offering and supporting many exploratory activities (LoS I & II).	6. Assisting in documenting students' activities and accomplishments.
7. Recognizing and responding to unique, high-level needs (LoS III & IV).	7. Assisting and supporting curriculum planning and individualized modifications.
8. Using many, varied materials and resources.	8. Collaborating in projects for instruction and staff development.
9. Collaborating with the LoS Catalyst.	9. Coordinating evaluation and public relations.

Figure 3: Classroom Teacher and LoS Specialist: Partners in Talent Development

It is important to recognize *what is within our control and what we might create by applying our imagination and energy,* and then to make every possible effort to discern and nurture every student's unique needs, interests, and potentials. It is equally important for schools to recognize *what is not directly within our control* and to serve as advocates and catalysts to locate, arrange, and support those opportunities for students. We must also provide time and opportunity for students to relate out-of-school activities and experiences to what is taking place in the school.

> *"It is likely that some combinations of the home, the teachers, the schools, and the society may in large part determine what portions of this potential pool of talent become developed. It is also likely that these same forces may, in part, be responsible for much of the great wastage of human potentiality."*
> —Bloom (1985, p. 5)

Through deliberate, sustained collaborative efforts, it becomes possible to enable and empower students to discover, develop, and express their strengths and talents. The challenges of working to nurture the strengths and talents of many students are not inconsistent or incompatible with those of serving students whose talents are already manifest at high levels. Rather, these goals support and affirm each other and lead us to a lofty vision and to high expectations for education. The challenge of providing a rich and varied array of talent development opportunities may seem formidable at first glance. In fact, however, it is not difficult to design a large number of options—perhaps even thousands of possibilities (see Figure 4)—when you consider many combinations of people, places, processes, and products. (Add your own ideas for Figure 4, too!)

Programming for Talent Development:
10,000 Possibilities

People	Places	Processes	Products
Physician	Shopping Mall	Problem Solving	Written Report
Lawyer	Zoo	Knowledge	Multimedia
Architect	Classroom	Analyzing	Drama/Play
Truck Driver	Playground	Evaluating	Painting
Engineer	Museum	Listening	Software
Musician	Restaurant	Hypothesizing	Video
Custodian	Theater	Interviewing	Music or Song
Inventor	Swimming Pool	Deducing	Legislation
Farmer	Sports Arena	Forecasting	Poem
Retailer	Hospital	Experimenting	Sculpture

Note. By adding just five more entries to each of the four columns, the number of possibilities increases from 10,000 to more than 50,000. Consider the exciting possibilities for building the strengths and talents of many students in many ways!

Figure 4: Thousands of Programming Possibilities

Given the challenge, the major purpose of this book is to provide a thorough but practical overview of the LoS approach to programming. We want our readers to understand both the "why" and the "how" of the approach. To those ends, the book deals with the rationale and description of LoS, and also provides practical guidelines and resources to support its implementation in the school setting.

This chapter presents the foundation for our LoS approach to programming for talent development. Chapter 2 presents an overview of the four levels of service. Then, each of the four following chapters (Chapters 3 through 6) describes one of the levels in greater detail. The final chapter presents information and resources to guide planning, implementation, and evaluation of LoS at the classroom, school, or district level.

A Rationale for Deliberate Talent Development Efforts

Modern educators, parents, and community leaders recognize that the expectations and demands made of today's schools are greater and more important than ever before in our history. As the complexity of our world increases, as technology expands our horizons and creates global opportunities for communication and collaboration, as the rate of change with which we must cope increases constantly, and as our children and youth face more and more difficult personal, career, and social challenges than any previous generation, the demands on education also increase.

We realize today that not only knowledge, but talent, imagination and creativity, critical thinking, problem solving, and good judgment are qualities far too important to be wasted or unfulfilled—now or for the future. We realize that education is a process that does not take place only within the walls or boundaries of a classroom or a school building (and, increasingly in the future, may not be limited to any single physical place). We recognize that talented accomplishments in many areas are essential to progress, our quality of life, and perhaps even survival. Home, school, and community all share in the responsibility for nurturing talent in many domains and dealing with many complex challenges in those domains. These include, for example:

- science, medicine, technology, and engineering, to find solutions to problems of hunger, disease, and the destruction of our living environment;
- leadership, social and behavioral sciences, and organizations, to respond to the issues of justice, inequality, diversity, and governance;
- arts, culture, and entertainment, to bring us new opportunities and to enhance and celebrate creative expressions that add joy and meaning to life;
- ethical and moral principles and philosophical analysis, to guide individuals and groups in understanding and dealing effectively with the most complex concepts and challenges of human existence; and
- personal fulfillment, enabling individuals to live in greater mental, emotional, and physical health and to celebrate their own talents, as well as those of others.

Talent development is closely and importantly linked, therefore, to today's concerns for educational innovation and improvement and to recent efforts to formulate and support high standards and challenging goals for all students. Talent development also represents deliberate efforts to incorporate and integrate the fundamental ingredients of success in personal effectiveness and productivity in many other areas of life: in one's hobbies, participation in civic or social organizations, volunteer work or service, and a wide range of other interpersonal situations. People in our workshops and presentations often tell us that the most important, meaningful, and sustaining experiences of their lives centered on their own personal creativity and talent development opportunities.

We may not be optimistic about our ability to assess and select those young people who display the greatest potential for significant accomplishments in these areas or in any other specific talent dimensions. In truth, these accomplishments often unfold over many years in an individual's life; talent development is truly a lifelong challenge. Talent *development* (which implies deliberate, systematic efforts to promote growth) is a complex challenge. It involves many factors and their interactions. These include a variety of specific experiences at home, at school, and in various settings in the community. We might think of talent development as a sometimes fragile ecosystem, rather than as a unitary and fixed set of educational activities or programs.

Growing numbers of educators, parents, and community leaders are coming to recognize that these are not issues of importance for only a few special students or in a few academic areas. Rather, they are challenges we must address for all students in all content or career areas and by all teachers, schools, and districts, as well as in the home and community. Increasingly, we must all deal with the responsibility of serving as important guardians of the future for all our students. Talent development is everyone's business in today's world.

Educators and others who are involved in talent recognition and development are called upon to make every possible effort to discern *every student's* unique needs, interests, and potentials, and to provide educational opportunities for their nurture. These efforts are directly and importantly related to the challenges of providing quality education for all students and for preparing young people to be successful in life (personally, as well as through their careers) in a rapidly changing world.

A number of underlying principles and beliefs influence us and serve as the foundation for our approach. These are based on contemporary theory and research from several areas of study, including cognitive and developmental psychology, educational psychology, educational administration, curriculum and instruction, and others. These underlying principles provide a foundation on which school practice can, and should, build. Exemplary programming for talent development is the result of careful planning, on-going review and analysis, and commitment to both innovation and continuous improvement. It does not come about by chance. Our approach is based on a set of 23 "fundamental tenets and beliefs." (You can obtain a complete statement of those tenets and beliefs from the Center for Creative Learning Web site, http://www.creativelearning.com, or by contacting the authors.) For our specific purposes in this book, six of those statements are particularly germane:

1. All students have worthwhile potentials and interests. Appropriate and challenging instruction can lead to significant achievement and satisfaction in at least one talent area for many students (or often more). Talents exist and may be expressed and developed in many important and worthwhile domains.

2. Some students show advanced levels of talent and accomplishment early in their lives. With sustained effort, encouragement, and support, many students will continue to pursue the development and expression of their strengths and talents and thus may eventually attain a high level of excellence and accomplishment.

3. Talent development is lifelong and fundamental to personal growth and healthy development. As children mature, previously unrecognized strengths and talents ("hidden potentials") often emerge, and talents may also become more specific, focused, and sustained.

4. Talent development occurs in an "ecosystem of development." Appropriate, challenging, and developmental programming also occurs in settings or through agencies outside the school and requires the commitment and support of the home and community, as well as the school.

5. Effective programming for talent development involves many and varied resources and levels of service. These support, extend, expand, or enhance, rather than supplant, the daily school program.

6. Appropriate, challenging, and developmental educational experiences are fundamental responsibilities of the school, not special privileges or frills.

Desired Outcomes for Students

The nature of talent and the many important and varied ways in which talents can be expressed and applied in life also influence our view of the important student outcomes that should result from deliberate talent development efforts. These desired outcomes are presented in Figure 5. They involve three broad categories: the healthy, effective person; the independent learner; and the creatively productive person. The three categories are interrelated and mutually supportive, forming a constellation of talent development outcomes (rather than independent or unrelated options) for all students.

Desired Student Outcomes
of Programming for Talent Development

Healthy, Effective Person

- Competent—Demonstrates mastery of basic skills
- Aware of personal styles or preferences and their implications for effective learning and productivity
- Personally and socially effective
- Thinks and reasons soundly and fairly
- Functions effectively in team or group settings
- Identifies and carries out effective leadership practices
- Confident in own abilities, commitments, and judgments
- Committed to lifelong learning and talent development

Independent Learner

- Sets goals and defines task or project outcomes
- Identifies methods and resources for meeting goals
- Carries out appropriate actions and activities
- Pursues projects and products with passion and vigor
- Monitors, manages, and modifies actions as needed
- Uses a variety of tools and technologies to design, produce, and share products
- Evaluates accomplishments and plans new directions

Creatively Productive Person

- Sees many possibilities or connections
- Looks at problems in varied and original ways
- Sustains and enhances existing strengths
- Innovates—Formulates new possibilities and directions
- Communicates ideas and shares products with others
- Expresses and acts on principles, values, and convictions
- Committed to improving the quality of life for self and others
- Confident and courageous in pursuing goals and purposes despite obstacles

Figure 5: Programming Outcomes

Institutional or Strategic Goals for Levels of Service (LoS) Programming

Given our view of talent, our rationale for the importance of talent development in modern education, and the desired outcomes for students, we can state a number of general institutional or strategic goals for deliberate talent development efforts or initiatives—for the home, school, or community. The goals of a contemporary LoS approach to talent development include the need or challenge to:

- keep student success and productivity in the forefront of policies, procedures, and actions;

- make deliberate efforts to seek, recognize, respond to, and enhance the development of students' strengths, talents, and interests;

- offer appropriate and challenging learning opportunities and experiences for all students;

- create, maintain, and support a culture for teaching and learning that values, promotes, and rewards excellence;

- create, support, and enhance an environment or climate conducive to developing, recognizing, and celebrating individuals' talents;

- recognize and honor individuality, helping all students to be aware of their learning styles and preferences, and providing opportunities for them to study, explore, learn, and perform in their best ways;

- incorporate creative thinking, critical thinking, problem solving, and decision making on a daily basis;

- encourage independent, responsible self-direction and teach the skills required for independent, self-directed learning;

- inspire individuals to become aware of (and to make optimal use of) their own strengths, talents, and interests—for their own benefit and for the benefit of others;

- use many and varied resources (people, places, and materials) to expand learning opportunities and enrichment for all learners;

- be a talent spotter on a daily basis—always alert for signs of strengths, talents, and interests in every person (Young, 1995);

- engage in on-going dialogue, learning, and communication to sustain commitments to innovation and continuous improvement.

When people in a school and community work together to address these goals, there will be "two-way benefits." The efforts that you make to design and carry out programming for talent development will strengthen the total school program; in addition, the work you do to strengthen your total school program will also "stretch" and challenge your gifted/talented programming efforts. Taken together, these mutual benefits lead to schools that are powerful, exciting, rewarding places for everyone involved in their work. The vision we hold for the schools of tomorrow is one in which there are high standards and expectations for all, but also in which there is excitement, engagement, and a sense of enjoyment about what takes place every day. Such a vision might be criticized by some as too idealistic; we do not believe progress results from setting goals and aspirations that are uninspiring. We've never heard of successful results from a campaign to "demand mediocrity."

Summary

In this chapter, we have provided a brief overview of the important goals for programming for talent development. The home, the school, and the community all play vital roles in developing students' strengths and talents. Programming for talent development will have important benefits and consequences for students, but it also enriches the lives of educators, parents, and many other people in any community. In the next chapter, we will begin to examine the nature and structure of effective, powerful programming for talent development.

References Cited

Bloom, B. S. (Ed.). (1985). *Developing talent in young people.* New York: Ballantine Books.

Young, G. (1995). Becoming a talent spotter. *Creative Learning Today, 5*(1), 4–5.

Chapter 2
Overview of the LoS Framework

This chapter will provide a brief overview of the LoS framework, highlighting each of the four Levels of Service. Chapters 3 through 6 will examine the four levels in much greater depth and detail; the purpose of this chapter is to provide you with "the larger picture" of the LoS framework. Each of these five chapters will begin with a story—a brief summary of an experience you might have if you were to visit a school or a classroom to observe the LoS framework in action. Approach the story as if we (the authors) were taking you on a short "field trip" to help you (the reader) see firsthand how LoS operates. The stories are based on our experiences in real school settings from a number of school districts in which we have worked over the last two decades. We've constructed these stories to illustrate some of the key ideas that you will explore in the chapter, and, of course, we have had to omit many of the richer details you would observe in a "live" visit in the interests of brevity and illustration. At the end of each chapter, we will return to the story to tell you more about it and to highlight its relevance to the chapter's main ideas.

An Inventive Thinking Program

The Happy Valley School District offered a districtwide inventive thinking program that spanned grades K–12. The "kick-off" event for the program was an assembly program, repeated in each school, with a presentation by a prominent local inventor whose work was also well known internationally. The inventor presented information about his background and the experiences that attracted him to inventing, shared specific experiences that related to his significant inventions, and answered students' questions about himself, his inventions, and the process of inventing. The talent development program coordinator had also developed a series of detailed inventive thinking curriculum activities and encouraged teachers to pick and choose from these lessons based on their specific interests and needs. Classroom teachers decided whether or not they wanted to participate in the inventive thinking program. The inventive thinking curriculum activities could be substituted for some portion of the regular curriculum; they were not extra activities to be added to an already full plate. The participating teachers decided where to fit the lessons into their classroom program, possibly in a unit in science (e.g., creating a device to keep things cool in a unit on energy conductors and insulators), social studies (e.g., American history, the 1900s and the Industrial Revolution), or language arts (e.g., units on advertis-

*ing or persuasive writing, or reading biographies of famous inventors).
The teachers then introduced the lessons to their classes (e.g., "Today we
are going to begin a series of lessons about inventive thinking. All of you
will have an opportunity to learn about inventors, inventions, and
inventing during the next few weeks. You will have a chance to acquire
some new problem-solving skills and to examine your strengths and interests related to this area."). They usually combined some of the inventive
thinking lessons with some of their own lessons and content.*

*Upon conclusion of the classroom inventive thinking lessons, the
teachers challenged their students to apply what they had learned: "In a
few weeks, our school building will have an Inventors' Celebration. I
know many of you would like the opportunity to apply what we learned
about inventive thinking. Please take home one of these invitations to
participate in our Inventors' Celebration and discuss it with your parents.
If you wish to participate in our celebration, follow the instructions provided regarding creating your own invention and bring your product to
school for sharing with other inventors on the day indicated by the invitation."*

*For the inventive thinking program, classroom teachers had the
option of requiring all of their students to produce an invention and participate in the Inventors' Celebration as a culminating and evaluating
activity. They also had the option of providing classroom time and assistance for students to create their products or treating product development as a homework assignment. The building-level Inventors'
Celebrations, which were held during the school day, were organized and
facilitated by teacher volunteers and the district talent development program coordinator. The format for these celebrations engaged students in
displaying their products, viewing the other displays, and participating
in dialogue with the other young inventors about their inventions and
the inventive process they followed in creating their products.*

*All students who produced a product for the Inventors' Celebration
received an invitation to continue working on their invention in order to
enter it competitively into the school district's Invention Convention.
Those who applied attended a mini-course scheduled as a pull-out class.
The class, taught by the district talent development coordinator, consisted
of a series of lessons designed to help students polish and refine their products. This mini-course incorporated practical strategies for communicating
their inventions to a real audience and tips for gaining the competitive
edge. As a culminating activity, the talent development program sponsored
a districtwide Invention Convention, which was held on a Saturday
morning and was open to the public. The staff encouraged families to*

attend together, and invitations were sent to the community through school district publications and local news media. The coordinator recruited judges, including several local businesspeople, legislators, and school board members. During the Invention Convention, the inventors explained their inventions to the public audience and made oral presentations to a panel of judges.

A team of students, parents, classroom teachers, and the coordinator planned additional, individualized opportunities for a few highly-motivated students who demonstrated exceptional strengths and talents in their project and who wished to continue pursuing their interest in inventing. For example, one student was connected with a mentor from a technical field related to the student's inventing interests. Other students researched procedures for obtaining a patent on their product. Several students developed and implemented marketing plans for their inventions, and a few even began to reap financial gain from their hard work. Sometimes, the students obtained the time and support to carry out their plans from classroom teachers, and at other times they were guided by their parents outside school hours.

Setting the Stage for Effective Programming

Effective programming enables us to find and develop students' strengths and talents simultaneously or to act at once as both talent spotters and talent developers. We concur with the observation made by Simonton (1997): "Genius is not just born; it is also made—by the environment in which talented youth emerge" (p. 341). The dynamic interaction between these two goals suggests that programming should be appropriate, challenging, and developmental. The meaning and implications of these three dimensions are summarized in Figure 6.

Appropriate	Challenging	Developmental
• Especially well-suited	• Invitingly provocative	• Designed to assist or encourage growth
• Consistent with needs and characteristics	• Arousing competitive interest, thought, or action	• Gradually becoming manifest or apparent
• "Fits" well	• Expanding, "stretching"	• Helping to bring about improvement
• Makes sense	• Forward-looking	• Making active and available
• Wisely and carefully-designed	• Capacity-building	• Enabling progress or advancement to new or higher levels
• Compatible	• Inspiring, stirs passion and intense involvement	

Figure 6: Essential Qualities of Effective Programming

If something is appropriate, it is "especially well-suited" to or compatible with an individual's needs or wants. When we refer to appropriate instruction for a student, we mean that it is consistent with the student's personal characteristics and needs, that it "fits" the student well, makes sense, and is wisely and carefully designed.

"Challenging" describes experiences that are, in Webster's terms, "invitingly provocative" or "arousing competitive interest, thought, or action." Challenging instructional experiences are energizing, stimulating, expanding or "stretching," forward-looking and capacity-building, exciting, motivating, and engaging. They are inspiring experiences that stir the learner's passion and promote intense and sustained involvement.

Developmental programming is designed to make students' unique characteristics active and available. Development involves making students' strengths and interests visible or manifest through a process of planned instruction and activities. Programming expands opportunities for constructing an essential foundation upon which to build more effective use of one's strengths and sustained interests, thus enabling them to develop into unique talents. We are confident that many of the essential elements of talent can, in fact, be nurtured through appropriate, challenging, and developmental programming experiences.

Many students are likely to reach the constellation of talent development outcomes presented in Chapter 1 (healthy, effective person, independent learner, and creatively productive person) when engaged in appropriate, challenging, and developmental programming experiences. Such experiences help students to acquire a rich knowledge base and engage in productive thinking at the highest and most complex levels for their age, achievement levels, and grade as their readiness emerges. Programming must also provide students with opportunities to apply and use substantive content in creative production. It is not just the knowing, but the doing that we must value. It is unlikely that anyone will invest sustained effort and perform at his or her highest capacity while engaged in experiences that are not appropriate and challenging. Who among us has not gone on "mental cruise control" when faced with a task that is much too easy? Likewise, haven't we all turned our engines off when overwhelmed by an overly difficult situation?

As proposed in our "fundamental tenets and beliefs," appropriate, challenging, and developmental educational experiences are basic responsibilities of an effective school. Furthermore, appropriate and challenging instruction leads to significant achievement and satisfaction in at least one talent area for most students, and, as Feldhusen (1998) observed, "[M]ost students have at least three or four relatively high talent strengths and their talents often are found in several of the four domains" (p. 29).

Spencer and Spencer (1993) found that the ability to develop others was one important factor distinguishing superior teachers from their average-performing peers. Their strengths included the use of innovative teaching methods, flexibility in allowing students to use individualized ways to learn or to meet requirements, and a genuine belief in students' potentials. The greatest distinction between superior and average-performing teachers was in the teachers' belief in the students themselves and the way these positive expectations shaped the teachers' feedback to the students. Less effective professionals were likely to write off at least some of their students by expressing negative expectations that, in turn, justified less effort by the teachers to develop the students' strengths. Some teachers even blamed the lack of student success on variables outside of their control, such as the home environment or student's ability. In contrast, the most effective performers expressed positive expectations for even their most difficult students. They held the belief that students can learn in spite of negative variables and they possessed confidence in their own ability to overcome any obstacles to student learning.

Superior performers also held themselves personally accountable for the learning of all children. As a result of their strong commitment to help all students learn, they identified their own weaknesses and shortcomings in order to seek assistance in those areas or to otherwise prevent those weaknesses from hindering their work. The most effective teachers demonstrated an intrinsic enjoyment of their work and a strong commitment to the process of learning and to the mission of their school.

Much like superior performers in general, "talent spotters and developers" (Young, 1995a-d) make a personal commitment to the principle that "all children can learn" by accepting responsibility for programming in which every student has the challenge and opportunity to discover and use her or his best potentials and talents and to develop those talents as fully as possible. This implies that it is essential for schools to recognize that many programming options must be sustained in an effective instructional program. Furthermore, when providing appropriate and challenging instructional experiences, one does not settle for poor or mediocre quality of performance. Teachers are often surprised when individual students rise to the challenge of high-level expectations once they are presented with appropriate and challenging opportunities.

One such example is illustrated by a talented bassoon player who seldom practiced playing her instrument until she became involved in a regional symphonic orchestra. When asked by her parents why they no longer had to nag her to practice, she replied that previously it had not been necessary for her to practice in order to perform her parts in the high school band program. Now, practice was much more important. The regional orchestra program only met once a week to prepare for a new public concert performed every 2 months. Since there were also other talented bassoon players in the symphony, she certainly did not want to look bad in front of them, the conductor, or the public. Clearly, her new opportunity was both appropriate and challenging, thereby motivating her to perform at a higher level.

In LoS, development implies active intervention, deliberate planning, and ongoing commitments to innovation and improvement, while programming is what people do to make development happen. The programs we create in school (or in any other setting) are not the important ends in themselves. As Bloom (1985) argued,

> "The characteristics required for a broad range of talent fields in modern society are such that a large proportion of individuals could learn well in one or more talent fields —if the conditions for their development are available in the homes, the schools, and other learning opportunities. Nothing is more central in our LoS approach to talent development than the importance of designing and providing appropriate and challenging experiences through which it becomes possible to bring out and build upon the best in every person." (p. 598)

Essential Attributes of the LoS Approach

The LoS approach to programming for talent development involves five essential attributes or elements. LoS programming is:

- **Flexible**. Programming is multidimensional, including many different people, places, and kinds of activities. It is not one formula, single curriculum, or set program of activities or services.

- **Inclusive**. Programming is appropriate, challenging, and developmental, and, thus, available for anyone. Programming includes a broad range of talents and does not serve just one fixed group of students. Services are program-driven, rather than identification-driven.

- **Responsive**. Programming responds to the positive needs of students. It guides planning and decision making and leads to modifications of instruction. The mission of programming is to design and deliver appropriate, challenging, and developmental instruction through which we can bring out the best in every student.

- **Proactive**. Programming challenges the teacher, school, district, parents, and community to take constructive actions for talent development. Taking initiative for talent development becomes everyone's business.

- **Unifying**. Programming provides a structure and terminology for communicating effectively about talent development within and among home, school, and community.

The Four Levels of Service

Effective programming that takes into account these characteristics and commitments is certainly not "neat and simple" in the school setting. It is much more complex and challenging than a fixed or "one-size-fits-all" program. LoS programming involves a wide array of opportunities or services to respond to students' unique strengths, talents, interests, and potentials. The activities might engage varying groups of students working with different leaders or instructors at varying times and even in a variety of places. It is essential, then, to organize these opportunities in a purposeful way. Figure 7 illustrates a broad framework through which many programming activities or services can be organized in a practical way.

Programming for Talent Development:
"Levels of Service (LoS)"

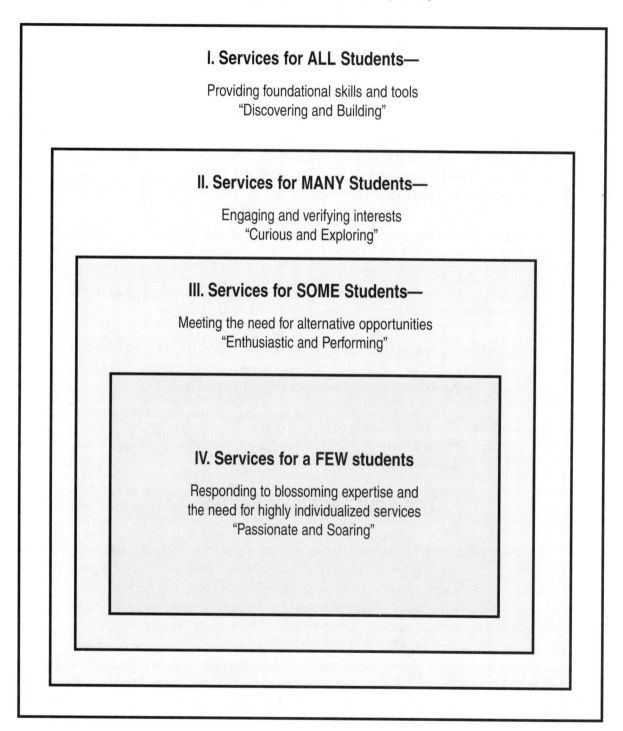

I. Services for ALL Students—

Providing foundational skills and tools
"Discovering and Building"

II. Services for MANY Students—

Engaging and verifying interests
"Curious and Exploring"

III. Services for SOME Students—

Meeting the need for alternative opportunities
"Enthusiastic and Performing"

IV. Services for a FEW students

Responding to blossoming expertise and
the need for highly individualized services
"Passionate and Soaring"

Figure 7: The LoS Framework

Levels I and II. These are the most inclusive dimensions of LoS. Levels I and II provide students with a variety of opportunities to explore many different talent areas. During their explorations, students will have opportunities for their specific strengths, talents, interests, and potentials to emerge and be recognized. Exploratory activities provide talent spotters with opportunities to recognize a special "spark" or potential that can be nurtured later. They also provide students and their parents with opportunities to discover areas of interest that can be nurtured outside of school.

The main distinction between Levels I and II involves who participates in the activities and services. Level I services involve all students. They are basic ingredients or elements of an excellent classroom instructional program. All teachers plan and carry out many Level I services routinely in their classrooms as part of their ongoing instruction. Level I services also include activities that might involve all students at a certain grade level (with the collaboration of several teachers) or even schoolwide activities in which all students participate. Level II services involve many students in a broadly inclusive way that might best be described as "invitational." For these services, any student might be involved, but not every student will participate. Level II services involve self-selection or voluntary enrollment based on individual interest and demonstrated competence for the specific activity.

Both Levels I and II focus on planned opportunities, often for group participation, that are part of the basic instructional program and are readily available to all students. These broad-based and highly inclusive services are intended to provide students with basic productive thinking skills and tools. They can also provide a foundation for more self-directed creatively productive learning. They are "exposure and exploratory" experiences through which students can begin to consider possible areas of interest. Activities at Level I and Level II serve as "building blocks" for more complex, sustained talent development activities and experiences.

Levels III and IV. Level III and IV opportunities differ from Level I and II opportunities in two important ways. First, the focus shifts from foundational group opportunities to small-group and individual opportunities that respond to the unmet needs of specific students. In our work, the term *needs* does not refer to deficiencies, impairments, or weaknesses, but to the demands and challenges that arise from one's strengths and talent potentials. Discussing the needs of students refers to educational responses that are necessary if instructional programming is appropriate, challenging, and developmental. The second difference involves the students' activities and participation. While any student might participate in Level I and II opportunities, educators look closely and specifically at an individual student's demonstrated and sustained strengths and interests to determine the appropriateness of particular services at Levels III and IV. The criteria they consider for student participation relate directly to the student's characteristics and background in that content area or talent domain.

In this brief overview, we have grouped Levels I and II and Levels III and IV. In practice, however, each level can occur independently; each one is important in bringing out the best in every student. It is also equally important to recognize that effective programming might also involve all four levels. In LoS, it is necessary to consider a full range of programming options. In this way, all students' strengths, talents, and interests may emerge and develop. In the LoS approach, then, there is no one formula, single curriculum, or set program of activities or services that will be offered to just one fixed group of students who have been "identified as talented."

Providing services only at Levels I and II ignores the unique needs of students with advanced levels of accomplishment or achievement in any talent area. Some schools contend that the needs of all students can (and should) be met only through provisions made by classroom teachers in the regular program. Such programs usually focus only on Level I and II services. This approach creates a situation in which schools offer "a little something for everyone," but fail to make any deliberate efforts to recognize or respond to the needs of students with specific high-level strengths and talents. Providing only a few specific services at Levels III and IV for a small, narrowly defined and identified group of students leads to providing too few services for too few students. The LoS approach views all four levels of service as important dimensions of comprehensive programming for talent development.

The following four charts summarize the unique qualities or elements of each of the four Levels of Service "in action," or in relation to the ways programming might actually be implemented at the school or district levels. The charts also identify the essential elements of activities or services for each level and describe important student characteristics and needs to consider at each level. Finally, the charts highlight some unique considerations for differentiating instruction at each level.

Structure and Dynamics for the
Four Levels of Service

Level	Unique Details	Essential Attributes of Programming	Student Characteristics and Needs	Emphasis in Differentiation
Level I: Services for ALL Students **Discovering and Building**	Appropriate and challenging content and process for all students Foundational skills and tools, exposure to talent or interest possibilities	• Offering a rich and varied array of opportunities to provide exposure to many topics, themes, or talent areas • Building a foundation for talent recognition and development, discovering areas of possible interest • Building on the recognition that all students differ in style, rate, pace, and format of learning • Making a commitment to balance process and content in curriculum and instruction • Engaging students in learning and practicing process tools • Offering activities that are generally brief in duration, readily accomplished in the classroom and/or through specific "events" outside the classroom (e.g., field trips, guest speakers)	• Knowing students' learning styles • Knowing students' creativity and critical thinking characteristics to determine process strengths and link to learning needs • Preassessing content skills for curriculum compacting	• Differentiation calls for all educators to recognize and respond to unique and varied learner characteristics • Differentiation involves deliberate instruction in productive thinking tools and metacognitive skills, as well as content

Level	Unique Details	Essential Attributes of Programming	Student Characteristics and Needs	Emphasis in Differentiation
Level II: Services for MANY Students **Curious and Exploring**	Invitational opportunities. "Anyone might; not everyone will" Engaging in and verifying interests and possible strengths and talents	• Allowing students to explore possible areas of strength or interest • Creating opportunities to stimulate curiosity and heighten anticipation • Including student-selected process or content activities or programs • Providing opportunities to practice process skills and tools • Enabling students to verify interests and possible talent strengths • Offering activities of specified scope and duration; may be brief (single session or multiple sessions over several weeks), but may also be extended over a longer period of time (e.g., during a semester or school year)	• Understanding, documenting student interests • Building student profiles or portfolios that reflect present interests and past experiences • Listening to input from parents, teachers, community leaders, peers, or the students themselves • Using anecdotal or performance data to learn about students' strengths and interests	• Differentiation driven by varied curiosities and interests of students, recognizing that all students need not participate in all activities or in any activity with the same degree of commitment and enthusiasm

Level	Unique Details	Essential Attributes of Programming	Student Characteristics and Needs	Emphasis in Differentiation
Level III: Services for SOME Students **Enthusiastic and Performing**	Services respond to needs based on individual strengths, talents, and sustained interests, even though they are often group-oriented activities (many of which are readily available in most school settings) Strengthening competence, confidence, and commitment in a talent area	• Drawing upon a number of existing options to meet needs, but using placement or selection based on specific data regarding individual student characteristics in relation to the content of the activities • Including advanced classes, honors classes, or AP courses in specific content or talent areas, as well as individual or group problem-solving projects or independent study projects • Making joint efforts among schools to ensure sufficient numbers of students to offer certain options • Participating in group activities or programs offered after school or during the summer (by the school or by outside agencies)	• In Level III and in Level IV, there is student selection, but it is based on the student's specific characteristics and "readiness," in relation to the skills that will be required for successful engagement in the activity • Demonstrated student interest and motivation to engage in the activity • Evidence of ability and/or achievement in the specific content or talent area • Characteristics and needs are clearly relevant to the content and performance expectations for the specific activity or service	• Differentiation involves offering varied activities or services, primarily group-oriented, on the basis of students' unique characteristics and needs • Differentiation also provides opportunities for real problem solving and inquiry that extend beyond "practice problems" or contrived situations

Level	Unique Details	Essential Attributes of Programming	Student Characteristics and Needs	Emphasis in Differentiation
Level IV: Services for a FEW Students **Soaring and Passionate**	Intensity of the "match" or linkage between the student's high-level needs and the unique programming activities that are constructed to respond to those needs Responding to the blossoming expertise of the student	• Targeting custom-planned, designed, or selected responses to the individual student • Often involving advanced, high-level, sustained services constructed specifically for a particular student • Providing resource people as guides or mentors for the student (may involve outside agencies) • Offering classes or group-based activities that involve an extensive shift of level or setting (e.g., elementary-age student taking secondary level course; middle school or high school student in a college course)	• Student demonstrates high level of competence, interest, and involvement in the content or talent area • Student likely to have exhausted all options available in existing school placement • Student very likely to have "track record" of involvement in activities or groups, or in independent research, inquiry, or performance, either in school or in outside organizations or events • Student demonstrates high level of ability and growing expertise in the content or talent area • Student is often very easy to "spot" by virtue of past and current activities and accomplishments	• Differentiation at an intense, personal, and highly challenging level for students with exceptional needs and evidence of high-level ability and passion • Element of "risk" in that goals, activities, and outcomes are not predetermined by the teacher or a curriculum guide • Requires creative effort and "stretching" one's thinking or problem solving

Figure 8 provides illustrative examples of activities or services for each of the four Levels of Service. Each of the following chapters will present and discuss additional examples for each level.

Levels of Service (LoS) Examples

I. Services for ALL Students—

Examples: Creative and critical thinking skills and tools, individual learning styles, field trips, guest speakers ...

II. Services for MANY Students—

Examples: Extended group projects, Destination ImagiNation®, Future Problem Solving, mini-courses, inventing programs or contests, science fair, special interest or hobby group ...

III. Services for SOME Students—

Examples: Honors or advanced classes, acceleration in classrooms or grade advancement, advanced programs at school or in the community, performing groups ...

IV. Services for a FEW students

Examples: Early admission, grade advancement, dual enrollment, early graduation, mentorships, advanced independent research or inquiry projects, internships ...

Figure 8: Summary of the Four Levels of Service

Program development begins by recognizing and building upon what services or opportunities for talent development already exist in the home, school, and community. It continues by exploring "the Four E's": expanding, extending, enriching, and enhancing learning as we create and carry out appropriate, challenging, and developmental learning experiences for all students. There are deliberate efforts: First, we consider ways to expand or to broaden the scope of the regular program. Second, we ask how we might extend or stretch learning for all students. Third, we consider what new opportunities might be created to enrich or increase the most desirable characteristics of talent in students. Fourth, we ask how might we enhance or improve the quality and increase the challenge of our total instructional program.

The challenge for the staff of a school is not to select one service or even a small group of services and opportunities as its "Talent Development Program," but rather to ask:

1. What services and opportunities do we already have in place? What are our programming positives?

2. What services and opportunities might be added? What is our wish list?

3. Of the services and opportunities not now available, which ones might readily be developed? What are our immediate "opportunity areas?"

4. In what ways might we expand the provisions we offer during the next 3–5 years?

5. How might we ensure that we are doing the best possible job of "linking" these options with the students who will benefit from them?

Some Frequently Asked Questions

Several questions arise frequently in discussions of the LoS approach. One of the most common questions is: *Do the four levels describe students with different levels of ability, talent, or giftedness?*

Our answer to that question has always been, and continues to be, "No!" The four levels describe services—programming activities or educational experiences—that schools can provide in different combinations and ways for different students (as appropriate and necessary) at different times. The levels of service describe multiple ways in which we might recognize and nurture students' strengths, talents, or sustained interests, not "kinds" of students or degrees of ability. We might speak of a student for whom Level IV activities are appropriate and challenging, but we do not speak of a "Level IV Student" as if that represented some categorical identity.

It is true that there are fewer students who, at any time and in relation to any activities or services, will be involved in Level III services and fewer still whose needs will call for a particular Level IV activity. By contrast, Level I activities reach all students, and Level II services involve many students. However, it is important to keep in mind that the number of students that any activity serves is not determined by a preset percentage or eligibility quota; rather, it is a reflection of the nature of the services themselves. As the services become focused more specifically on characteristics and readiness in relation to a specific talent area, the number of students for whom any activity is appropriate will change. Educators do not start out by saying, for example, "We can only permit 2% of our students to be served at Level IV." Instead, as they observe specific characteristics and needs in a student that can best be met through Level IV services, they will take the steps necessary to provide the services.

Another common question is, *"Are the four levels sequential, so that students should be expected to move or progress from one level to the next, through all four levels?"*

For any particular student, based on his or her specific strengths, talents, and needs, there might be involvement at all four levels, and work that students do during their involvement in activities at any of the Levels of Service might be a catalyst or "springboard" for involvement in services at other levels. An individual student might, during the course of several weeks, months, or even years, participate in programming at all four levels. However, is it not necessarily the case that there must be a sequential progression from one level to another, that the levels must depend on each other in an hierarchical way, or that any student might require services at all four levels. Linking students and services always focuses on recognizing students' specific strengths, talents, and needs and then responding in ways to ensure that instruction will be appropriate, challenging, and developmental.

The next frequently asked question is: *"Why are all four levels relevant to gifted/talented programming? Aren't Levels III and IV the points at which it really becomes 'gifted' programming?"*

Each of the four levels of service involves a unique and important way of differentiating instruction in relation to students' strengths, talents, and interests. For that reason, all four levels contribute in important and essential ways to the school's overall talent development efforts.

Level I provides skills and tools that create an important foundation for talent development, such as creative thinking skills (and tools for generating options), critical thinking skills (and tools for focusing options), Creative Problem Solving, and basic research or inquiry skills. The skills and tools all students learn in Level I will contribute to their ability to recognize and deal with opportunities in areas of their strengths, interests, and talents over time. Level I also involves assessing and clarifying students' personal characteristics, interests, and learning style preferences and helping parents, teachers, and the students themselves to understand their strengths and to clarify the ways in which they can "be their best." Level I activities expose students to many different topics and experiences, creating a starting point for clarifying and developing strengths, talents, and interests.

Level II involves opportunities for students to explore themes, topics, or talent areas about which they have an initial curiosity or for which they demonstrate interest or aptitude as observed by parents, teachers, or others. Level II activities provide students with experiences that may be deeper, more challenging, or sustained over a longer period of time (in comparison with the brief duration of Level I activities). Through their involvement in Level II activities, students can put their skills and interests to the test, confirm or disconfirm their interest in future work in a specific area, or identify other new directions (or "spin-off" possibilities) to pursue. At the same time, Level II activities can be sufficiently finite in duration that students are not required to make a long-term commitment to an area that might not really hold promise for them or sustain their interest and enthusiasm.

In these ways, we see both Levels I and II as a "staging platform" for the emergence and development of specific talent areas for any student. They are essential to the overall talent recognition and development process because they can help create or clarify promising opportunities and directions for students to pursue.

Levels III and IV, in which the focus shifts to linking students with programming opportunities based on their unique needs and characteristics, represent services that are clearly related to our traditional approaches to "gifted programming." However, it is important to recognize that the services students need often build on Level I and II experiences. The Level I and II activities may also provide an excellent "window" for discovering or observing needs for Level III or IV services. It's also important to keep in mind that the selection of students for activities in Levels III or IV is based on specific characteristics and needs for the activities, rather than on global scores (such as an IQ "cutoff" score).

The Rest of the Story ...

The story of the inventive thinking program at the beginning of this chapter provided an example of all four levels of service carried out within a single thematic area. It illustrated ways in which the LoS model can cut across various content areas. It also offered an example of the importance of involving the school, the home, and the community in effective programming for talent development. The story also demonstrated how the LoS framework can be used to respond to the emerging needs and sustained interests of students over an extended period of time. In this program, students were not required to participate hierarchically or sequentially through the four levels each year. Their participation depended upon their demon-strated competence and commitment within the domain of inventive think-ing. The schools also provided a number of other different services in addition to inventive thinking at each of the four levels as part of the dis-trict's total talent development program. Not all opportunities offered in the district necessarily extended through all four levels of service.

Each of the four levels of service responded to the emerging interests and talents of the students. The opportunities became more individual-ized based on the students' performance and interests throughout the inventive thinking program. The talent development program supported their efforts with a series of lessons and appropriate teacher orientation to the program. The initial Level I opportunity—the guest inventor's assem-bly program—provided an awareness experience for all students. The fol-low-up work was conducted in the regular classroom, but it was not just "dumped" on the classroom teachers. The classroom teachers' involvement at Levels II through IV was beneficial, but voluntary and less direct than at Level I. The building level Inventors' Celebration (voluntary and based on interests) represented Level II. Level III included the invitational mini-course and the culminating invention convention. Level IV included sev-eral advanced activities that were highly individualized. Parents, support staff, and community resources all supported the regular classroom teach-ers and the students at each level of service. The classroom teachers were not expected to do the job alone!

The specific opportunities described in the story were created and implemented to respond to the recognized needs of the students. These opportunities evolved as part of the school district's efforts to implement a flexible, inclusive approach to talent development. Effective program-ming in the LoS approach involves many opportunities to recognize, respond to, and nurture both the readily visible talents and the emerging strengths and talents of students.

References Cited

Bloom, B. S. (Ed.). (1985). *Developing talent in young people.* New York: Ballantine Books.

Feldhusen, J. F. (1998) Developing student talents. In D. J. Treffinger & K. W. McCluskey (Eds.), *Teaching for talent development: Current and expanding per-spectives,* (pp. 27–34). Sarasota, FL: Center for Creative Learning.

Simonton, D. K. (1997). When giftedness becomes genius: How does talent achieve eminence. In N. Colangelo & G. A. Davis (Eds.), *Handbook of gifted education.* (2nd ed., pp. 335–349). Boston: Allyn and Bacon.

Spencer, L. M., & Spencer, S. M. (1993). *Competence at work: Models for superior performance.* New York: Wiley.

Young, G. (1995a). Becoming a talent spotter. *Creative Learning Today, 5*(1), 4–5.

Young, G. (1995b). Celebrating creatively productive outcomes. *Creative Learning Today, 5*(3), 6–7.

Young, G. (1995c). Responding to and nurturing talent. *Creative Learning Today, 5*(2), 4–5.

Young, G. (1995d). Talent spotting: A practical approach. *Creative Learning Today, 5*(4), 6–7.

Chapter 3
Level I: Programming for All Students

After an illustrative story, this chapter presents four important "keys to success" in carrying out Level I of the LoS approach. We offer several illustrations and examples of Level I in action and provide examples of Level I services in various settings, content areas, and grade levels.

Ms. Jackson's Social Studies Class

Ms. Jackson is a dynamic middle school social studies teacher. This story summarizes observations that actually took place in her classroom over a 2-week period.

Ms. Jackson introduced a unit on state government by exploring what the students already knew. As part of this process, she asked them, "Why should you care about state government?" One student answered, "We will have to pay taxes in the future and we should know what this stuff is all about." Another said, "I've never thought about this." Ms. Jackson seized upon the last comment and asked the students to work in small groups to develop a list of interesting questions. After 20 minutes the groups reported their questions to the whole class. Ms. Jackson recorded their questions on sheets of flipchart paper and then displayed the sheets for everyone to see.

She instructed the students to review and analyze each question carefully to see if they could group them into common themes. Several students expressed surprise when they noticed that the questions fell into four areas: the structure of government, the way the branches of government work together, key political figures, and current issues.

The teacher told the students that she expected them to work alone, with a partner, or in a group, to research one of the four areas. Each individual would be responsible for knowing and applying the information. Several groans filled the air. Ms. Jackson smiled and reassured them that she would work closely with them during the entire unit.

Ms. Jackson introduced a center that contained a variety of resources. Among these were primary source materials such as copies of the State Constitution, maps, and autobiographical data. Secondary source material included history texts, political journals, and audio/visual resources. After she gave the class an overview of the material, she mentioned that they were welcome to use the media center. For those who wanted to do research on the Internet, she provided a list of useful Web sites and suggested that the students investigate others that might add depth to their topics. At this point, the teacher told the class that their initial tasks were to choose a topic and create a plan for doing their research. Ms. Jackson invited the students to consider the four topics and the questions in each of them, look through some of the resources, and then talk with others with whom they might want to work. Spirited discussion followed.

In the next class session, the teacher asked the students if they had any additional questions. Alicia asked, "If I can contact the office of our state representative online and if she responds to some of my questions, may I ask her to come here and speak to our class?" Rob followed with, "I would like to do a search of the daily newspapers to find out who the key politicians are and what issues they support. Could you help me do it? And, would it fulfill my requirement for this unit?" The teacher responded positively and enthusiastically to their questions and invited students who might have additional thoughts or topics to meet with her.

They were eager to get started, and all but five students clustered together in small groups. As Ms. Jackson moved from group to group, she sensed that most of the groups were well on their way to delineating their topics and designing their projects. Then she was able to spend more time with each of the five individuals. She prodded their thinking by asking questions such as, "What would you like to learn? How might you accomplish this? Would you like to work by yourself, with a partner, or in a small group?" Three of them decided to work independently, and the other two decided to work together.

As the unit progressed, the students conferenced among themselves and moved back and forth between the classroom and media center. They challenged one another over the accuracy of details and conclusions. They questioned one another, discovered previously unknown resources and information, took notes diligently, and seemed to be having a good time doing it. One group had a difficult time with the wording of the State Constitution, specifically with the section that dealt with the structure of the Judiciary. Students from another group offered to "double team" that section with them.

Once their research was complete, the class reconvened to discuss and evaluate their efforts. Ms. Jackson taught them a specific thinking tool to use (the ALoU tool) for focusing their ideas. They were to frame their comments in positive terms citing the advantages (A) and uniqueness (U) of the process and results. Then, they would express their concerns or difficulties in question form, stating them as limitations (L) that might be overcome (o) in future projects (e.g., "How might we obtain more primary source materials?").

The students' last challenge, Ms. Jackson explained, was to present their information to the rest of the class in varied, unusual ways that drew upon their unique strengths and talents. She shared a few examples of ways that previous students met this challenge. These examples triggered a stream of chatter as the students immersed themselves in the challenge!

The story of Ms. Jackson's class did not end with classroom presentations. She was so proud of her students and their work that she asked for and received permission to invite parents, friends, and community leaders to witness and celebrate their accomplishments. The students organized and presented an evening program titled "Our Amazing State Government."

What can you learn from your visit to this classroom? Ms. Jackson's class illustrates many of the basic concepts and principles of Level I in the LoS approach in action: activities and services you can provide for all students on a consistent basis. In this chapter, we will guide you in planning and carrying out Level I in your own classroom, school, or district.

What Are Level I Services?

Level I services are activities, learning experiences, or instructional experiences that help to expand and enhance learning for all students—every day, in every classroom. They are essential ingredients to any high-quality educational program. Level I services serve to "raise the bar" for all teachers and students. Establishing high standards and expectations for all students leads to engaging every student in appropriate, challenging, and developmental learning opportunities everyday.

Level I services most often take place in the classroom setting. While these services might involve several people, the classroom teacher usually has primary responsibility for planning, organizing, and delivering them. Level I activities typically include readily accessible resources and a specific, but brief time frame. They are deliberate and carefully planned experiences that can usually be delivered to more than one student at a time.

These broad-based, highly inclusive, and readily available services provide all students with rich and varied knowledge and skills—in relation to both curricular content and productive thinking or "process" tools. Level I services often serve as a springboard for subsequent self-directed, independent learning experiences and for a variety of other team or group projects and activities. In addition, Level I services provide opportunities for students' strengths, talents, interests, and potentials to emerge and be recognized or affirmed by the students themselves and by others; for this reason, we describe Level I as a stage of "Discovering and Building" through services that lay the foundation for talent recognition and development.

Even though Level I services center around activities in the classroom, they can include involvement and collaboration among many and varied people and they can extend to a variety of places, resources, or settings outside the classroom. Therefore, in carrying out Level I, teachers remain alert for opportunities to draw on the contributions of parents or community members who, through their workplace expertise and their personal interests and hobbies, can extend, enrich, and enhance Level I activities. Level I activities are high in "hands-on, minds-on" involvement or engagement, and they suggest words like *doing, applying, producing,* and *sharing,* not just words like *sitting, listening, watching,* and *reciting.* Level I services help students in constructing meaning and developing a rich foundation of content knowledge and process tools.

All students should have many and varied Level I opportunities. Do not treat these as "special privileges" that should be offered to only a few students, and do not use them as rewards (or withhold them as punishments) for classroom performance or discipline purposes. Effective Level I services are inclusive, enjoyable, and stimulating experiences that contribute to a positive climate or environment for strengths, talents, and interests to be explored and celebrated by all. They help you to construct a foundation for future in-depth talent development activities.

Rationale and Purposes

Let us consider two important fundamental questions about this level (and, in the following chapters, about all four levels): What is the rationale for Level I services in our approach to programming for talent development? What purposes do Level I services have in relation to the overall goals for programming?

- **Discovery and Exposure.** By providing Level I services in any classroom and throughout a school or a school district, educators help students to discover their interests and experience new areas in which they might have (or might develop) strengths. Level I services offer opportunities for students to sample various areas or topics for themselves.

- **Motivation and Stimulation.** The emphasis on active involvement and high levels of engagement and participation are "hooks" for motivating students. By participating in Level I activities, students often discover new opportunities and challenges they never realized could be exciting and rewarding to pursue.

- **Foundation for Extended Learning.** Level I services provide the essential foundation of challenging content (in academic or curricular areas and in other interest-based learning areas) that are important to success in today's world of "accountability for results." In addition, Level I services provide process and learning management skills and tools that students can use as the foundation for higher level learning projects and experiences. Level I activities involve a balance between content and process, in which students learn and practice using process tools (e.g., tools for generating ideas or tools for focusing their thinking), as well as content skills and knowledge.

- **Elevation of Quality.** Level I services help teachers to "raise the bar" of challenge and engagement for all students in every classroom. They give students interesting and engaging challenges to which they might rise to new levels of success and productivity. Schools today hold high standards for all students, and many expectations that were once only thought to be appropriate for only a few students are now applied on a much broader and more inclusive basis.

- **Locate Hidden Strengths.** When students have broad access to many and varied kinds of interest development or enrichment opportunities, both they and we may find strengths that were not apparent in any other way.

- **Self-Management.** Through involvement in Level I services, students will also have new opportunities to learn and apply skills for managing and directing their own learning.

- **Enjoyment.** When students express a high level of curiosity and motivation, they can be a real challenge for teachers. With large classes and many students who need extra time and effort for basic learning success, it can become too easy to overlook the needs of high-performing students (e.g., "Well, they're doing okay; they don't need any extra help"). When students persist in their questioning, they can even seem to become a nuisance to the teacher. Maintaining an active and varied array of Level I services helps to keep student engagement and on-task behavior high across all levels of performance, making the daily classroom experience more enjoyable for everyone.

- **Variety.** "One size does *not* fit all." By offering a variety of Level I activities, teachers can increase the likelihood of finding opportunities to capture and build upon the interests and curiosity of all students. Recognizing the many ways in which students differ from each other and responding in varied ways to those unique attributes are cornerstones of Level I. Recognizing that students differ considerably in their interests, personal characteristics, and learning style preferences builds a strong foundation for differentiated instruction.

Implementing Level I Services for All Students

There are four important "keys to success" in implementing Level I programming. You will not do them all at once or in a fixed sequence. You will likely find it to be most efficient to work on some of them concurrently. To implement Level I, it is crucial to think about the way you approach your entire class, rather than about students in predefined categories or groups. We hope that you will find that you are already doing many of the things listed and will simply be able to gradually add to or expand your classroom programming. Talents, strengths, and sustained interests must be sought. Students cannot show them if opportunities are not provided for them to be discovered or expressed. All four "keys" fit together and may even overlap in an effective classroom. The four keys to success for Level I are summarized in Figure 9.

Keys to Success in LoS Programming: Level I

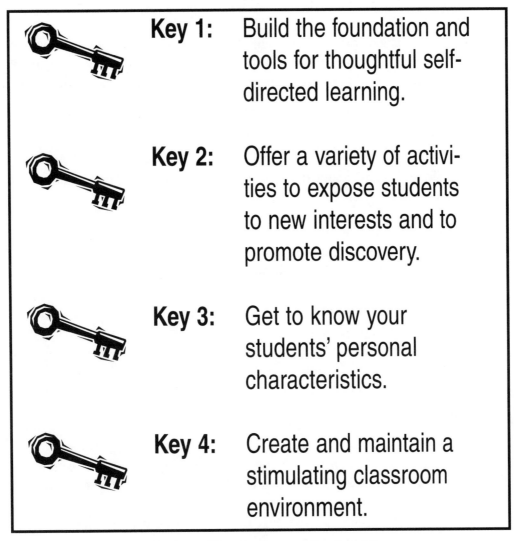

Key 1: Build the foundation and tools for thoughtful self-directed learning.

Key 2: Offer a variety of activities to expose students to new interests and to promote discovery.

Key 3: Get to know your students' personal characteristics.

Key 4: Create and maintain a stimulating classroom environment.

Figure 9: Keys to Success for Level I

Key 1: Build the foundation and tools for thoughtful, self-directed learning.

This key deals with the ways in which you help students to become thoughtful, self-directing learners. Building the foundation focuses on "transportable" skills, tools, and processes that are essential for becoming a productive thinker and effective learner in any content area. In Level I, you will make deliberate efforts to provide students with instruction in areas associated with productive thinking, metacognitive thinking, researching and communicating information, and in managing one's own learning. In Level I, building the foundation involves:

- Teaching students specific guidelines and tools for creative thinking (generating ideas) and critical thinking (focusing ideas), using both everyday life experiences and curriculum-related activities.

- Asking questions that call for higher level thinking (beyond recognition and recall of correct answers); teaching the students to ask challenging questions of themselves and each other; and applying appropriate "wait time" in discussion.

- Teaching students specific problem-solving methods designed to be applied in different contexts.

- Teaching students about decision making and providing opportunities for them to practice and apply their learning.

- Providing opportunities for debriefing and processing of learning activities. Teach students to monitor, manage, and modify their thinking during learning and to reflect on the process and outcomes after a learning experience.

- Teaching students to "talk with themselves" about their own work, to engage in reflection and self-assessment, and to monitor their own growth and change over time. Involve them in managing the documentation of their own products and accomplishments, as well as in keeping records (scrapbooks, learning portfolios, or journals) for tracking their own progress.

- Working with students to establish high expectations for quality work. Engage them in assessing and documenting quality work by teaching them how to give and receive feedback in constructive ways. Practice evaluation skills through evaluating their own work and that of other students through peer evaluation.

- Encouraging students to take charge of their own learning by helping them to learn how to set appropriate and challenging goals for their learning and plan how to accomplish those goals.

- Creating opportunities for students to learn, use, locate, and share a variety of technologies and learning media on a day-to-day basis.

- Teaching and practicing a variety of presentation and communication skills that incorporate visual, auditory, and kinesthetic modalities.

Key 2: Offer a variety of activities to expose students to new interests and to promote discovery.

This key deals with the ways in which you help students to discover exciting new possibilities or directions. It involves creating opportunities for them to sample or try out a variety of disciplines, topics, ideas, concepts, issues, and events. These "exposure experiences" allow talents and interests to emerge and be recognized by teachers and students. They stimulate new talents and interests that students might wish to pursue in more depth later. Sometimes, existing or even hidden talents and interests are sparked through exploration. In Level I, exploration and discovery involves:

- Providing time, opportunities, and a variety of resources in the classroom for students to explore and pursue their own curiosity.

- Encouraging students to "play with ideas" and explore unusual questions and possibilities.

- Providing interest-centered opportunities that extend beyond the regular curriculum.

- Involving parents, older students, and community resource people in teaching and learning activities and projects in your classroom.

- Utilizing community resources such as museums and businesses by not only taking field trips, but by also finding ways to bring them into the classroom.

- Listening to students and parents for areas or topics suitable for exploration.

Key 3: Get to know your students' personal characteristics.

This key deals with the ways in which you take deliberate steps to recognize and respond to the many and varied ways that students learn and demonstrate they are learning. Our broad conception of talent includes sets of characteristics or traits that can be nurtured or enhanced. Each cluster involves many skills that can be developed through instruction. When expressed and focused in a particular direction and when recognized and nurtured through appropriate instruction and guidance, these skills and abilities become the foundation for creative, productive behavior. Personal characteristics include one's cognitive dimensions, personality factors, motivational dispositions, and style preferences. In Level I, knowing your student's personal characteristics includes:

- Gathering both formal and informal data about the talent strengths and special interests of all students and seeking ways to build on them every day.

- Looking closely at students' content knowledge and skills in order to prepare for curriculum compacting (freeing students for alternative activities to take the place of instruction in areas they have already mastered).

- Gathering both formal and informal data about students' learning style strengths and preferences and using those data to provide variety at any given time during the day.

- Using a variety of teaching and learning strategies and resources to promote active involvement and participation by all students.

- Helping students to explore and discern their own interests, strengths, talents, and style preferences.

Key 4: Create and maintain a stimulating classroom environment.

This key deals with the ways in which you organize the physical space and material resources of your classroom. It includes the efforts you make (yourself and with the involvement of the students) to create a classroom that is "learner-friendly" or conducive to varied activities by individuals or groups of varied size. The classroom environment also encompasses your choices and decisions about how you manage and deliver instruction to accommodate diverse strengths, styles, and interests. It involves considering how you establish a climate for inquiry and active involvement, including the use of hands-on, minds-on instructional methods that engage students in high-level learning. In Level I, a stimulating classroom environment includes:

- Involving every student in challenging opportunities every day and exposing them to a variety of new themes, topics, questions, issues, and challenges.

- Organizing your classroom so various students can work, individually and in small groups, on different and varied activities at any given time during the day.

- Providing many and varied opportunities for all students to demonstrate their ability to use or apply their learning through a variety of projects and products.

- Planning instruction that involves many and varied student activities and groupings within the classroom.

- Providing opportunities for students to create a variety of products and share them with appropriate audiences and through appropriate outlets.

- Providing varied learning resources encompassing people, print materials, and technology/media-based materials.

- Encouraging students to help and support each other, to learn with and from each other, and to work individually and cooperatively on tasks in order to advance both individual and group goals.

An initial step in implementing Level I might be to examine your current classroom practices in relation to these four keys. Begin by asking yourself, "What am I already doing well? What are some areas that I want to learn more about?" Explore some of the activities listed below and gradually expand Level I programming in your classroom throughout the school year.

Illustrative Examples of Level I Services

Specific Level I services in any school will vary from one teacher or teaching team to another. They may also vary from one grade level to another, across various content areas, among school buildings, and from one district to another. We cannot provide a single, fixed set of "official" Level I services for all levels or school settings.

However, we can provide several specific illustrative examples of Level I services organized around the four keys. These examples cover a variety of grade levels and content areas. They are drawn from our experiences over the past two decades in working with teachers and schools using the LoS approach.

Use these examples as part of your planning process for talent development programming. The Planning Guide at the conclusion of this chapter will help you to examine what kinds of Level I activities and services you are already offering. Remember that you do not have to carry out these activities alone and that you will not (and, reasonably speaking, cannot) do all of these things at once. We do encourage you to assess your "current realities" and to plan constructively for enhancing and extending your programming over a period of time. (The time period might vary widely from one school or school district to another because of the differences among settings we noted above.)

Key 1: Build the foundation and tools for thoughtful, self-directed learning.

Example: In a middle school classroom, the teacher discovered that most of the questions in the science book chapter on the circulatory system were simple recall. She developed alternate questions that emphasized the higher levels of Bloom's taxonomy, such as analysis, synthesis, and evaluation.

Example: An elementary teacher changed the way he asked questions in his class. His daily routine included questions that called for students to demonstrate productive thinking, predicting or forecasting, decision making, and communicating their own ideas.

Example: In a primary classroom, students searched through old magazines for pictures of things that were orange. They cut the pictures out and pasted them onto a large pumpkin outline. Over the course of the month of October, they added more pictures, working to obtain at least 50 different pictures by Halloween.

Example: In a high school English class, before reading a new novel, students worked in small groups with the brainstorming tool for generating ideas to create a list of questions to guide their reading.

Example: A high school English teacher asked her class to read a short story. Afterward, she presented statements and asked the students to judge whether each was true, false, or uncertain. The students had to explain their thinking and support their views with evidence from the story.

Example: A middle school teacher had his students analyze editorials from the newspaper to determine which statements were fact and which were opinions. Some students wrote editorials that were totally opinion-based. Others wrote editorials in which their opinions were supported by facts. The entire class then critiqued and discussed the products.

Example: An elementary teacher used Creative Problem Solving (CPS) with her class to help organize the necessary props for a class play. They determined which props were needed, where they could find them or how they might make them, and who would do what to ensure that the props were ready in time for their performance.

Example: Four times during the year in a middle school social studies class, students were required to research one aspect of their social studies curriculum. Students produced independent projects to demonstrate the results of their research. For example, one student conducted extensive research on the Second Continental Congress and the Declaration of Independence. Then, he pretended that he was a delegate and used the ALoU thinking tool to consider the possible advantages of declaring independence, the limitations of the idea and how those limitations might be overcome, and the most unique features of the declaration. Finally, he wrote a short essay stating how he would have voted and why based on his analysis of the idea.

Example: In an elementary class, students learned how to conduct interviews to collect research information. They practiced developing questions and conducting interviews in their classroom. Then, they interviewed a guest who came to their classroom and wrote an article for their school newspaper based on the information they gathered.

Example: In an elementary classroom, students worked together to develop a list of criteria for "What makes a good toy?" They then worked in groups to create a toy and used their list of criteria to evaluate the results.

Example: In a high school mathematics class, students worked with the teacher to create a rubric for evaluating their solutions to given problems. They then worked in small groups to solve the problems. Each group presented their solution for one of the problems to the whole class; the students used their rubric to evaluate their work and solutions.

Key 2: Offer a variety of activities to expose students to new interests and to promote discovery.

Example: In an elementary school, all students participated in two 6-week-long sessions of an activity period. Students chose from a variety of exploratory topics. Everyone on the school staff (teachers, clerical help, custodians, teaching assistants, and administrators), as well as parents, community volunteers, and central office administrators were involved in presenting to small groups of students.

Example: In an elementary school classroom, a local stockbroker explained investing to the students using a book called *A Money Adventure*. Students then participated in a stock market simulation activity.

Example: In a middle school classroom, the teacher encouraged all types of learning experiences and diversity of interests. She had her students interview each other to discover things they were learning and doing outside the school setting. The information obtained was then discussed with the whole class and displayed in summary form on a "Learners Bulletin Board" as a visual reminder of their many and varied interests.

Example: In an elementary classroom, the teacher used the KWL technique to help prepare her students for studying a new topic. They identified what they already knew; what they had some ideas about but needed some clarification; and what they wanted to learn about the topic. She then used this information to guide her teaching and monitor student learning.

Example: In an elementary classroom, the teacher created a "hands-on/minds-on" learning center, composed of odds and ends collected by the teacher and students. The teacher encouraged the students to manipulate the objects, generate questions, and pose challenges for others.

Key 3: Get to know your students' personal characteristics.

Example: In a middle school, the staff wanted to get more information about their students' interests, strengths, and personal goals. They decided to move fall parent/teacher conferences to the third week of the school year and change the format from "telling" to "listening." Because the purpose of these early conferences was to learn more about students' interests, they invited them to participate in the conferences with their parents. The staff, with the help of their gifted programming specialist, composed a letter that they sent home explaining the new concept. They also included a checklist to help parents and students consider specific activities and characteristics. During the conferences the teachers listened, asked questions, and took notes. The individual conferences concluded with all participants agreeing on a few general goals for the school year and identifying student, parent, and teacher responsibilities in relation to the action plan. Feedback from the conferences indicated that parents and students appreciated the opportunity to share information and become more active participants in the education planning. Teachers discovered that they were able to get useful information about the students in a more timely fashion and learned some things that they may never have discovered otherwise.

Example: In a high school, students were required to create and maintain cumulative exit portfolios. At the beginning of each semester, teachers guided their students through a review of their portfolios. This process helped teachers to learn about each student's strengths and career goals. The students and teachers then worked together to establish growth plans for each course.

Example: In a middle school, all students responded to the Dunn and Dunn Learning Style Inventory (LSI). After their responses were scored, the teachers, students, and parents received reports of the results. The school conducted information sessions for teachers, students, and parents to help them understand and apply the results.

Example: In a high school team-taught block class that combined social studies and English, students responded to VIEW: An Assessment of Problem Solving Style to determine their problem-solving style preference. The teachers held a debriefing session with students to help them understand their strengths and preferences during problem solving. They invited parents to a special evening presentation at which they also had the opportunity take the VIEW assessment and receive a debriefing. The staff encouraged parents and students to discuss their personal strengths and preferences with each other.

Example: A high school chemistry teacher offered students a number of options for proving they understood the concepts presented. Students could give a summary of each chapter's content through oral explanation; take a teacher-made written test; submit a written report, drawings, and diagrams; or conduct a teacher-approved, but student-selected, independent project.

Example: In a middle school math class, students received both visual and auditory input through use of an overhead projector. They were allowed to work alone, with a partner, or in small groups to solve problems and check their work.

Example: In an elementary school, teachers pretested all students at the beginning of the year using a series of cumulative skills tests they designed in the areas of mathematics, spelling, and reading. The teachers were able to use the test results to differentiate instruction for all students. In addition, they tested the students periodically to ensure that they were mastering skills as they were taught.

Example: In a middle school, students evaluated their progress as learners during each marking period. On their own separate report card, which accompanied the teacher's evaluation, students reflected on their progress and areas for improvement. There was also a place for them to make comments about their own educational growth plans. Parents were asked to sign both the teacher's and student's versions of the report card.

Example: In a high school English class, each student selected a famous creative adult to read about. They discovered characteristics about these people that made them different, but also made them special and talented. Students discussed their own personal differences and uniqueness.

Example: In an elementary classroom, students kept journals in which they wrote about their interests and reflected on their strengths and growth. The teacher did not grade or edit their journals, but responded in dialogue form.

Example: In a middle school classroom, students chose a "fantasy career" such as rock star, President, or CEO. They listed all of the things they associated with that career. Next, they investigated the realities of training, opportunities, benefits, and lifestyles involved through interviews and research. They then compared their initial perceptions of the career with its reality.

Example: In an elementary classroom, guest speakers representing career areas related to topics of study visited the class. For example, when rocks were studied, a geologist visited the class to discuss his profession.

Key 4: Create and maintain a stimulating classroom environment.

Example: In a high school science class, students worked in several ways based on individual choice. Some options were: working in groups of four to develop an underwater living unit, working alone writing a research report, and building a model or mobile. Each activity carried certain point values for grading purposes.

Example: In an elementary school's intermediate-level team, several students served as "experts" on specific pieces of audio-visual equipment. They posted a list of their names with each piece of equipment. Whenever anyone on the team needed to use the equipment, they checked the list of "experts" and consulted those students for assistance and support. The team of experts also prepared laminated instruction cards for the equipment to help ensure that the equipment would be used properly.

Example: In a middle school, students were introduced to the *National Geographic Index.* Using back issues of *National Geographic* magazine, students went on a "scavenger hunt" to track down various authors, articles, and resources. This activity was followed by a trip to the school media center to learn about using the *Reader's Guide to Periodic Literature.*

Example: An elementary teacher worked with his students to develop criterion checklists for rating independent study projects. After each student presented his or her project to the class, the other students filled out one of the checklists. For later projects, the students developed checklists independently.

Example: In an elementary school, students worked on spelling in heterogeneous study groups. Each week, the students worked together to learn the words for the test. Students received their own individual score and a team average score. The team with the highest average received a reward ticket for the following week.

The Rest of The Story ...

Ms. Jackson used Level I activities to help build the foundation for thoughtful, self-directed learning. She presented her students with a variety of tasks, provided examples of each, and checked to make sure that everyone understood what they were to do. Effective questioning helped students to clarify and expand their thinking. Students modeled this technique among themselves and when they needed additional teacher assistance. Finally, Ms. Jackson gave the students the opportunity to work with a variety of resources and then taught them a thinking tool, ALoU, to evaluate the process. Each of these teaching and learning activities provided the students with skills and strategies that would help them become self-directed learners.

Through Level I opportunities Ms. Jackson also created a classroom rich in exploration and discovery. Her students learned that she valued their ideas and opinions. She gave them the opportunity to investigate new or unusual topics and to access many and varied resources beyond the classroom. She provided time and encouragement for this to happen.

Further, Ms. Jackson used this unit on state government to get to know her students' personal characteristics. She promoted the active involvement and participation of all her students. She listened carefully to their questions and encouraged them to pursue their own ideas. She monitored their work and motivated them to use their strengths. She worked one on one with a few students to help them identify an area of interest for their research.

Finally, Ms. Jackson created and maintained a stimulating classroom environment. She encouraged students to use a variety of learning resources, including people, materials, and technology. They could choose the way they wanted to approach their research by working alone or with others. She allowed them to help each other when they had problems and encouraged them to tap into the strengths of others. They were able to demonstrate their learning in creative ways to a real audience. Ms. Jackson managed to design and deliver a unit of instruction that incorporated all four keys to Level I.

LoS Level I Planning Guide

We suggest that you make four copies of the Planning Guide (Figure 10), one for each of the four important "keys to success" in Level I of the LoS approach. Fill in each of the three columns to help you understand the areas where you are now most successfully implementing Level I (which we call "Programming Positives"); the areas that you are not now doing or not doing very much, but can easily implement soon (the "Opportunity Areas"); and the steps that will require much more time and effort to implement in your class (your "Wish List").

Then, consider the form in Figure 11. Once again, make copies for each of the four "keys." Begin by considering your Programming Positives, then the Opportunity Areas, and, finally, the Wish List. Set a target date for taking some steps to help you sustain your Programming Positives, and for taking action on the Opportunity Areas. Make some notes about how you will start them and carry them out, when you plan to begin, what materials or resources you will need, and how you will know that they're successful.

Finally, for each of the items on your Wish List, ask what first steps might help you to make some progress toward implementing them. What are some concerns or obstacles that might be holding you back and what might you do to overcome or eliminate them? Who might offer you some initial support for your efforts? What other resources might you locate to obtain some help in initiating them in your classroom? Which ones might be the highest priority items for you to start working on?

Programming Positives	Opportunity Areas	Wish List

Figure 10: Level I Planning Guide (Page 1)

Programming Positives	Opportunity Areas	Wish List
Who		
What		
When		
Where		
Why		
How		

Figure 11: Level I Planning Guide (Page 2)

Chapter 4
Level II: Programming for Many Students

After an illustrative story, this chapter presents five important "keys to success" in carrying out Level II of the LoS approach. We offer several illustrations and examples of Level II in action and provide examples of Level II services in various settings, content areas, and grade levels.

Math Enrichment at Smith Middle School

At the beginning of the school year, Mr. Brown, the gifted programming specialist (GPS) at Smith Middle School, and the math teachers in grades 5 and 6 met as a team to plan for student participation in a national mathematics competition. The competition consisted of five monthly contests, each having five challenging problems for students to complete within a given time limit. Individual students and grade-level teams earned awards based on the number of problems they solved correctly.

The team decided that Mr. Brown would do an introductory lesson in all math classes to explain the logistics, content, and required commitment. The lesson included a review of creative/critical thinking skills, examples of problems, and experience with the competition format. Teachers told their classes that all interested students could participate, although no one was required to do so. They strongly encouraged students in the above-average math classes to participate. They told the students that their contest scores would not have any effect on their grades.

After Mr. Brown presented the introductory lesson, the team scheduled a weekly follow-up lesson for the 120 students in above-average math classes. The lessons were led by the GPS with assistance from the classroom teacher and continued until the competition began in November. Eighty-five other interested students also met with Mr. Brown on a weekly basis, usually during team time or study hall. During these lessons, the classroom teachers and the GPS taught or reinforced math content, metacognition, creative and critical thinking skills related to math, and problem-solving strategies. The students usually explored sev-

eral strategies and reasoning methods they might use to solve the prob-
lems. The teachers engaged the students in discussions, to compare and
choose strategies to help them reach solutions. In addition, the GPS
placed a learning center in each classroom with creative/critical thinking
activities and additional practice problems.

The GPS and the math teacher administered and scored the monthly
contests. The day after each competition, they reviewed the results with the
students, giving special attention to the strategies that worked.

What might you learn from this story? It illustrates many of the basic concepts and principles of Level II of the LoS approach in action—activities and services you can provide for many students on a consistent basis. In this chapter, we will guide you in carrying out Level II services in your own classroom, school, or district.

What Are Level II Services?

Level II of the LoS approach involves a broad array of services for many students. Level II services are open and inclusive; any and all students might be able to participate in them. However, we do not expect that every student will participate in any specific Level II service. We use the simple phrase "Any student might, but not every student will …" to remember this major distinction. It may also be helpful to remember the descriptive phrase "Curious and Exploring" to characterize the unique focus of Level II.

Many Level II activities take place in the regular classroom, but they might also occur outside the classroom setting. They can be delivered or supported by someone other than or in addition to the classroom teacher. Level II services focus on enrichment and extension of experiences and provide opportunities for strengths, talents, interests, and potentials to develop.

Although both Level I and Level II services provide students with opportunities to explore a wide variety of talent areas, the opportunities in Level II are often longer in duration or deeper in involvement than the exploration and awareness that occurs in Level I. Level II activities may emerge from Level I programming, but they may also be derived from a student's special interests or previous experiences. In Level II, students actively choose to participate, whereas in Level I, the teacher initiates activities for all students.

Rationale and Purposes

Why do we include Level II in our approach to programming for talent development? What purposes do Level II services have in relation to our overall goals for programming?

- **Invitational.** By invitational, we mean that Level II services provide students with opportunities that they select or for which they are nominated by another person. Self-selection happens when students are drawn to an activity because of the challenge it offers. Nominations by other students, staff or parents occur for a specific reason; the perceived match between the nature of the activity or service and the background, readiness, and interest of the student. Typical comments one might overhear are: "This would be a really great and exciting opportunity for you ..." or "Knowing what I do about your interests, you can't afford to pass this up!" Invitational services create opportunities to recognize students' curiosities and interests and to use them to good advantage in recognizing possible strengths and talents.

- **Voluntary.** The students make a choice to participate. They have some ownership; that is, they have the interest and curiosity in the subject matter and are willing to invest some time in pursuing that interest. They express a curiosity and willingness to engage in the service and accept the responsibilities associated with participation. By providing voluntary opportunities, it is possible to draw students into seeking and exploring their strengths and talents, creating a foundation for expanding self-direction and self-management.

- **Deeper Exploration.** Students can "test the waters" or begin to extend their knowledge, deepen their understanding, and become more focused in a specific area of interest. Participation in Level II activities challenges students to acquire or develop new skills, try out their ideas, expand their involvement in areas of their strength and interest, and apply their learning. Level II activities provide a starting point for engagement in challenging talent development activities. Through Level II activities, students have opportunities to investigate an area and to verify whether or not it is an area or topic they are really motivated to pursue in the future; they can be a "testing ground" for talent development. Level II services also provide opportunities for students to apply and practice a variety of process skills and tools within the scope of the school setting and with adult support and guidance.

- **Short-Term: Finite Scope and Duration.** Level II services are more than one-time events such as might occur at Level I. The activities are short-term, but can vary in duration. They might be offered, for example, one period a day for one week or once or twice a week for one month or longer. Level II activities can stand alone and do not necessarily lead to continuing work by the student. Students must know and be willing to devote the required amount of time to the activity; Level II services offer them an opportunity to examine their commitment to follow through with such responsibilities.

- **Flexible Offerings.** Level II services vary from year to year, school to school, and place to place. They include a variety of topics that may depend on the specific interests and needs of students and the particular resources available in the school at that time. They may also take place outside the academic curriculum and in the community.

- **Emphasis on Discovery and Capacity Building.** Level II services provide opportunities for students to engage in activities that will give them and their teachers feedback about their interest and ability in a particular talent area. They provide information for informally discovering students' strengths and interests, stimulating the students' curiosity, and heightening their sense of eagerness and anticipation for learning about a topic. Level II services can serve as a "springboard" for continued, in-depth, individual, or group investment in a particular area, topic, or talent domain, opening up avenues and directions that might continue and expand at Levels III or IV. As noted above, they can also be opportunities for the student to discover that an area is not one that he or she will pursue further. Level II can provide opportunities for experiences that help students "hook" or "unhook" to future experiences.

Implementing Level II Services for Many Students

There are five important "keys to success" in implementing Level II programming. Level II services may be developed in response to observed strengths, interests, or needs of students in a particular classroom, in several classrooms, or across several grade levels. You will likely find that your school already provides many opportunities that can be classified as Level II programming services. As you review the keys, think about what you are already doing and about what else you might do in or beyond the classroom to provide appropriate experiences for students at this level. The five keys to success for Level II are summarized in Figure 12.

Keys to Success in LoS Programming: Level II

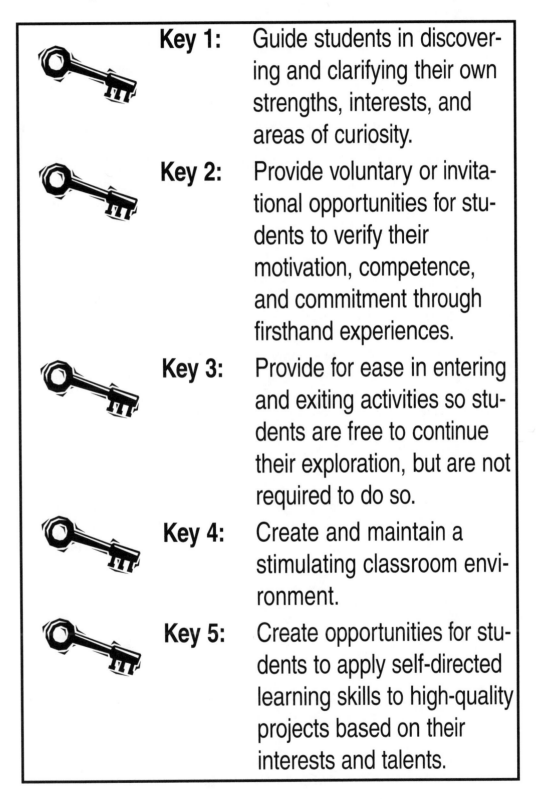

Key 1: Guide students in discovering and clarifying their own strengths, interests, and areas of curiosity.

Key 2: Provide voluntary or invitational opportunities for students to verify their motivation, competence, and commitment through firsthand experiences.

Key 3: Provide for ease in entering and exiting activities so students are free to continue their exploration, but are not required to do so.

Key 4: Create and maintain a stimulating classroom environment.

Key 5: Create opportunities for students to apply self-directed learning skills to high-quality projects based on their interests and talents.

Figure 12: Keys to Success for Level II

Key 1: Guide students in discovering and clarifying their own strengths, interests, and areas of curiosity.

This key deals with the ways in which you enable your students to understand and explore their personal strengths, talents, and interests. It is important for students to learn to become active participants and partners in recognizing and developing their own talents. Level II experiences help students, teachers, and other adults to identify strengths and interests. To guide students, encourage them to ask and answer such questions as: Do I have the motivation, curiosity, and desire to investigate and discover? Do I have potential in this area? Can I nurture this potential? What skills and knowledge do I already possess? What skills and knowledge do I need to develop to be successful in this activity? These questions can also guide you in observing and gathering data as students participate in any Level II activities. In Level II, preparing students to explore their strengths involves:

- Listening to input from parents, teachers, community leaders, peers, or students themselves and reviewing them with the students to help them recognize their strengths and talents.

- Using student interest inventories or anecdotal data.

- Initiating, continuing, or expanding learning style assessments and using the results to help students know how to study and work most effectively.

- Discussing or debriefing Level I activities to help clarify interests.

- Engaging students individually and in groups in conversations or discussions of interesting people, themes, issues, or events.

- Providing opportunities for students to "dig deeper" into curricular topics that hold special appeal or interest for them.

- Using curriculum compacting and lesson scaffolding to differentiate instruction.

- Talking explicitly with students about what they do well.

- Beginning to build student profiles or portfolios to clarify and document the students' strengths, interests, accomplishments, and products.

Key 2: Provide voluntary or invitational opportunities for students to verify their motivation, competence, and commitment through firsthand experiences.

This key deals with the ways in which you enable and support students in exploring and experimenting with their emerging strengths, talents, and interests. In Level II, a student self-selects an activity based on his or her interests or participates as a result of someone else's suggestion. The students have some ownership; that is, they make a choice to participate based on their interest and curiosity in the subject matter and their willingness to invest time and effort in pursuing that interest. By expressing their willingness to engage in the activity, they accept the responsibilities associated with participation. Services are usually group activities with numbers that vary depending on student interest and the resources available. The activities provide realistic experiences in a talent domain so students develop skills and see real-world connections.

Level II activities serve as a source of feedback for students and teachers about each student's strengths and interests in a particular talent area. The students have the opportunity to extend their knowledge, "try on" an area and test its "fit" for them, and to deepen their understanding of a topic. In Level II, providing students access to services involves:

- Knowing and listing many enrichment activities available in your school and pointing out promising opportunities to students.

- Letting students know about special activities, events, or programs in the school, district, or community.

- Holding individual or group talent planning conferences with your students.

- Nominating students to participate in activities.

- Being provocative! Setting out challenges before the students, and holding them to high standards of excellence.

Key 3: Provide for ease in entering and exiting activities so students are free to continue their exploration, but are not required to do so.

This key deals with the ways you guide students in initiating, continuing, or discontinuing their involvement in activities. Level II activities are helpful for students in discovering and starting things they want to do and sustain. Level II services are more than a one-time event, so students need to be willing to devote the required amount of time to the activity. Students need to have a clear picture of the requirements beforehand since the duration of the activities might vary considerably. The students must be able to assess whether they have enough interest to sustain their involvement for the necessary amount of time. If they decide to participate in an activity, they need to understand and accept the obligations involved. Level II activities help students to recognize and verify emerging passions.

Level II services also help students "put away" things they thought they might want to do, but learned through their initial participation are not really engaging or interesting. Some students might discover that completing a Level II activity has provided them with all they need to know about a topic. They might discover that they don't want to invest as much time and effort that continuing in that area would demand. In Level II, providing for ease in entering and exiting activities involves:

- Providing for open enrollment when possible.

- Making clear the expectations that accompany any activity and setting a specific process for entering or leaving the activity.

- Teaching students how to identify and use criteria for selecting and discontinuing involvement in an activity.

- Holding group discussions with students (and parents) about determining when it is appropriate to select or drop an activity.

- Not penalizing students when they make appropriate decisions to discontinue an activity that does not really match their needs and interests.

- Helping students to be proactive and to make thoughtful and deliberate decisions.

- Challenging individuals to look past easy, convenient options.

Key 4: Use a variety of school and community resources to enrich and enhance students' learning experiences.

This key deals with how you locate and use a variety of resources to carry out, expand, and extend programming. Asking questions can help you decide which school and community resources you need in order to advance student learning. Some questions might include: What activities are already offered within a classroom or the school that enrich and enhance students' learning experiences? Do these experiences cover a wide variety of subject areas and interests? What are some interests students have for which activities need to be developed?

You can also survey and investigate community resources to become familiar with what is available to meet student interests and talents. Combine your knowledge of students (their strengths, interests, and talents) and community resources to expand opportunities for talent development. In Level II, using school and community resources involves:

- Encouraging the involvement of all school personnel.

- Developing working relationships with community resources.

- Starting a "talent development opportunity" file in your school or classroom (possibly with PTA assistance).

- Speaking with community groups about providing opportunities for student involvement and participation.

- Developing a school- or districtwide community resource program.

- Creating and maintaining a list of student, staff, parent, and community volunteers who have specific skills, talents, hobbies, or expertise to share.

- Inviting many people to supplement curricular offerings by volunteering their time and sharing their talents.

Key 5: Create opportunities for students to apply self-directed learning skills to high-quality projects based on their interests and talents.

This key deals with how you provide students with tasks and challenges to practice and apply self-directed learning skills. Activities should include goal setting, planning, problem solving, evaluation, presentation, and record keeping. Level II involves designing your objectives so that your students can apply self-directed learning skills to independent projects and activities. In Level II, helping students to extend and apply self-directed learning skills involves:

- Using contracts or learning agreements to help students learn how to manage, monitor, and modify their choices.

- Making decisions and maintaining appropriate documentation of their work and products.

- Creating opportunities for students to present and share their work in various ways and for varied audiences.

- Guiding students in developing, selecting, and using criteria to evaluate their own work and that of other students.

- Providing opportunities for students to use appropriate equipment and technology to achieve their goals.

Illustrative Examples of Level II Services

As we noted about Level I in the previous chapter, it is also true in Level II that the actual, specific services that will take place in any school will vary by teacher or teaching team, by grade level, by content area, or among schools or school districts. We cannot provide a single, fixed set of "official" Level II services for all grade levels or school settings.

However, we can provide several specific illustrative examples of Level II services organized around the five keys. These examples cover a variety of grade levels and content areas. They are drawn from our years of experience in working with teachers and schools using the LoS approach.

Use these examples as part of your planning process for talent development programming. The Planning Guide at the conclusion of this chapter will help you to examine what kinds of Level II activities and services you are already offering. Remember that you do not have to carry out these activities alone and that you will not (and, reasonably speaking, cannot) do all of these things at once. We do encourage you to assess your "current realities" and to plan constructively for enhancing and extending your programming over a period of time. The time period might vary widely from one school or school district to another because of the differences among settings we noted above.

Key 1: Guide students in discovering and clarifying their own strengths, interests, and areas of curiosity.

Example: In a schoolwide inventing program in an elementary school, more than 85% of the students developed an idea for an invention and carried their idea through to a prototype that was displayed at the school's Invention Celebration. For many of the students, this was their first opportunity to create and display a product that would be viewed by many other people. Many parents, other relatives, and interested people from the community attended the Invention Celebration and had opportunities to talk with students about their ideas and products. The project provided opportunities for many students to discover and clarify their strengths and interests.

Example: In a middle school, the gifted programming specialist, a technology teacher, and a science teacher met with interested students before or after school several days a week for 3 months to work on various events for the Science Olympiad competition. Students selected events based on their strengths and curiosity. Some students were chosen for a team, which created opportunities for them to pursue advanced projects (and to engage in Level III of the LoS approach).

Example: In many schools, at the elementary or middle school levels, students may take instrumental music lessons. When they have reached a certain proficiency level, the music teacher invites them to participate in the school band or orchestra. Schools often provide similar opportunities in vocal music areas, such as chorus.

Example: In a middle school, the sixth grade students completed the Learning Styles Inventory, received their results, and discussed ways to capitalize on their preferences. The teachers and counselors met with small groups to discuss effective ways to do homework and ways that groups with similar preferences might build on their strengths when they were working on special projects or enrichment activities.

Example: After a field trip to a local art museum, the second-grade teacher discussed the experience with the class. Many students talked about their favorite works of art. The classroom teacher asked the art teacher to meet with those students in small groups based on their interests. The students learned more about the artists and their work.

Example: A high school math teacher noticed that the Fibonacci Number Sequence and its frequent appearance in nature intrigued many students. She developed a learning center containing reading materials, research questions, Web sites, and experiments. Interested students were encouraged to use the center and share their findings with her.

Key 2: Provide voluntary or "invitational" opportunities for students to verify their motivation, competence, and commitment through firsthand experiences.

Example: Most schools, at all grade levels, offer a variety of school clubs or extracurricular activities in areas such as art, drama, library, AV aides, computer, chess, foreign language, gardening, rocketry, magic, video, model building, woodworking, or photography. These activities provide engaging opportunities for students to explore and discover possible strengths and talents.

Example: A fifth-grade classroom teacher worked with a small group of students who created a box of artifacts representing their geographical area. They exchanged boxes with a class in another state. Using the artifacts in the boxes as clues, they identified the location of their partner class. This activity provided a "hands-on, minds-on" opportunity for many students to investigate their interests and talents in a number of different content areas.

Example: As part of an optional "mini-course" series in a middle school, a group of 20 sixth-grade students participated in a 10-week distance-learning course on sign language. At the end-of-the-year school assembly, they signed the pledge of allegiance. Other mini-courses included storytelling (which culminated in a school storytelling festival), a young authors program, a debate group, and a Web site design team.

Example: Teachers in a high school art department developed a monthly calendar of new exhibits at local galleries and colleges, presentations by guest speakers, community workshops and classes, and TV programs. The teachers shared the calendar with their classes. Feedback from students and parents was positive, with many attending the events and watching the programs.

Example: At the elementary, middle, or high school levels, many students have opportunities to participate in competitive team-oriented Creative Problem Solving programs, including, for example, the Destination ImagiNation® program (http://www.destinationimagination.org) and the Future Problem Solving Program (http://www.fpsp.org).

Example: A high school English teacher nominated students to participate in a mock trial competition. The teacher acted as a talent spotter looking for students with strong reasoning, verbal, and writing skills. Several students attended the training sessions and were selected for the school team, which placed second in the county competition.

Example: The opportunity to participate in a science fair can serve as a Level II activity for many students. Science fairs offer appropriate and challenging learning opportunities for students to search for an idea for an original project or experiment, conduct the project, document their results, and share them. Participating in a science fair can also serve as a springboard for more advanced work for some students. As a Level II experience, we believe that science fairs should, in general, be an invitational activity—for students who have a project idea or are motivated to find and develop a topic—rather than a required activity for all students.

Example: A school district's PTA group sponsored the National PTA Reflections program, inviting interested students in grades K–12 to submit original work in literature, music composition, photography, and visual arts.

Example: The gifted programming specialist in a middle school organized student participation in the local levels of the National Geography Bee and the National Spelling Bee. Many students enjoy studying and preparing for these annual competitions.

Key 3: Provide for ease in entering and exiting activities so students are free to continue their exploration, but are not required to do so.

Many Level II activities provide opportunities for students to explore topics or areas that they have never experienced before. The students can use these activities to determine their future participation in similar activities. For some students, the brief experience they obtain in a "mini-course" or special activity may lead to extended and advanced study, while for others, the initial activity may be sufficient. Any of the examples we have given above can be planned and conducted in a flexible way to accommodate this sense of exploration, discovery, and verification. Mini-courses, for example, give students an opportunity to experiment and discover; but, when they are over, some students will have had as much experience as they desire. Student participation in clubs or extracurricular programs also varies in relation to each student's motivation, interest, and active engagement.

Key 4: Use a variety of school and community resources to enrich and enhance students' learning experiences.

Although educators—and many parents, too—often think about programming for talent development in relation to activities that are organized and conducted in the school and by the school staff, many community-based organizations are also good examples of Level II services.

Example: During a unit on the 1960s, a high school social studies teacher realized that many students expressed interested in learning more about the Vietnam War. He contacted a local veterans group and found several veterans willing to share their experiences with the students. During study hall periods over the next few weeks, the veterans met with interested students in small groups to discuss the issues surrounding the war.

Examples: Community-based organizations might include Boy Scouts, Girl Scouts, Indian Guides, Camp Fire Boys and Girls, Boys and Girls Clubs, the Y's, 4H, Future Farmers of America, Junior Achievement, youth programs sponsored by fraternal or service organizations, and religious youth organizations—any of which can provide engaging, appropriate, and challenging learning opportunities for children and youth.

Example: Visitors who present school assembly programs for all students can also extend their impact by providing follow-up opportunities for small groups of interested students to meet with them; these can be excellent Level II activities. Many schools participate in visiting artist or visiting author programs. These can also be valuable Level II Activities. For example, in anticipation of a visit by a local author, a group of students read the author's books, made informational presentations to classes before an assembly, and then met with the author for in-depth interaction.

Example: In many communities, galleries, museums, science centers, or children's museums offer after-school, weekend, or summer experiences for students to pursue areas of interest and enjoyment. National programs, such as the Camp Invention program (http://www.Invent.org) provide engaging, enjoyable programs for students to learn about science, creative thinking, and inventing.

Example: A group of middle school students decided to plan and conduct a campaign in their school to make students aware of the importance of community service by young people. They wanted to build interest by sharing information about service projects in their community in which the students could volunteer. They developed a list of questions, contacted agencies to get answers to the questions, observed and worked as volunteers, developed a presentation and hand-out that included information about three agencies, and scheduled presentations for students. Their presentations were highly successful, and more than 25 other students in the school became involved in volunteer work in the community.

Key 5: Create opportunities for students to apply self-directed learning skills to high-quality projects based on their interests and talents.

Many competitive team Creative Problem Solving programs, contests, and academic competitions place considerable emphasis on challenging students to be independent and resourceful in defining a project or problem, conducting research, locating resources, formulating their own solutions, and developing their own project reports or presentations. These Level II opportunities help students to build and apply many self-directed learning skills, working on realistic problems and challenges that build motivation, process and learning-to-learn or metacognitive skills, and self-evaluation.

The Rest of the Story ...

At the end of the math competition, the teachers organized an awards assembly. One-hundred ninety-five students, approximately half of the fifth- and sixth-grade students, completed the five contests and received certificates. Seventy-five students scored in the top 20% nationally and received patches. Nineteen students ranked among the top 10%, and three students scored in the top 5%. The 19 students earned silver pins, while the 3 earned gold pins. The student with the highest score on each grade-level team received a trophy. One student achieved a perfect score and received a special medallion as a reward. All four teams from the school scored in the top 20% nationwide, and two of the teams were in the top 10%. After the assembly, the teachers placed the grade-level awards in the school's trophy case.

Involvement in this competition exposed students to higher level math concepts, improved their thinking skills, and rewarded them for their commitment and achievement. Several students discovered they liked math more than they thought they would. Because of their newly found motivation and effort, they improved their math grades.

Eighteen students with high scores and obvious interest accepted an invitation to participate in a Level III math activity. Students worked together to solve daily math problems and entered their solutions into a regional competition.

During the competition, Mr. Brown gave all the math teachers a monthly print-out of the contest results. From these print-outs, the teachers learned a lot about their students' thinking processes and math ability. They used the results of the competition to refine student placement in appropriate math classes.

Mr. Brown and the classroom teachers incorporated all five keys for success in this Level II programming service.

LoS Level II Planning Guide

Schools need to have a climate that encourages, validates, and actively searches for ways to include many Level II opportunities. Use the "Current Reality" chart (Figure 13) to summarize and document the "Programming Positives" in your classroom or school. Then, use the "Desired Future State" chart (Figure 14) to outline your "Wish List."

Area	What's Our Current Reality?
Surveying student interests and learning styles	
Survey of staff, parent, community interests (for possible mini-course)	
Community resource survey or data base	
Enrichment in content areas	
School-based clubs	
Contests, competitions	
Collaboration with community agencies	
After-school, weekend enrichment opportunities	
Summer camps	

Figure 13: Level II Planning Guide (Page 1)

Area	What's Our Desired Future?	
	Easy Areas to Add to Our List	Additions That Will Require More Work
Surveying student interests and learning styles		
Survey of staff, parent, community interests (for possible mini-course)		
Community resource survey or database		
Enrichment in content areas		
School-based Clubs		
Contests, competitions		
Collaboration with community agencies		
After-school, weekend enrichment opportunities		
Summer camps		

Figure 14: Level II Planning Guide (Page 2)

Use the following questions to help you implement Level II services:

- "Given our resources, what are some special opportunities that we are well positioned to offer?" Then, see what students rise to those opportunities!

- Given the student's interests, do we have the resources? If not, how might we obtain them?

- Ask "How might we …," rather than saying, "We can't because …" (Educators need to be problem solvers to respond to a variety of needs for which resources do not seem to be available.)

- Are opportunities communicated effectively to students and parents?

- Are expectations clear?

Parents also need to buy into enabling resources. They can help the school search for and provide services. They should be encouraged to volunteer their own time and talents. Parents can help by providing resources and opportunities out of school (learn from the example set by sports parents). They can help the school find emerging strengths in their children. Parents can assist and support the school in setting and maintaining expectations for LoS to occur.

Chapter 5
Level III: Programming for Some Students

"Our team has exhausted all our resources. This student needs a higher level of challenge than we can provide." These or similar words are expressed to gifted and talented program specialists, counselors, or administrators when a student needs Level III opportunities. Level III is the appropriate stage for students whose needs extend beyond the regular curriculum. Level III activities are the gateway to specialization. In this chapter, we will look closely at Level III, which is designed to offer challenges to some students.

We begin the chapter with an illustrative story, followed by a description and rationale for Level III services. Then, we present four "keys to success" for implementing Level III of the LoS approach and we offer some examples of Level III in action from various content areas and grade levels.

Story: Programming for Kevin

West High School's talent development program included among its many curricular offerings Advanced Placement courses, opportunities for interning at local businesses, and participation in competitive programs in a variety of content areas. The faculty and students were rightfully proud of their outstanding program designed to challenge academically competent students. Each year prior to the start of school, the gifted and talented programming specialist reviewed records of the incoming students. Her goal was to flag those whose programming needs might exceed the standard curriculum. She would then work with appropriate staff to gather information to substantiate this and finally design an appropriate and challenging program.

This year, Kevin Martel was one of the students who caught her attention. Kevin's records revealed exceptional achievement and interest in science. This young man distinguished himself in grades 6, 7, and 8 in a variety of ways related to science. Three years in a row he entered the science fair and demonstrated his talents in highly original projects. His projects on global warming, juvenile diabetes, and nutrition were very informative and creative. He earned several awards and numerous acco-

lades. His middle school science teachers and the gifted and talented programming specialist documented their collaborative efforts to compact the curriculum and summarized the advanced work he completed.

The high school team was energized by Kevin's potential and eagerly embraced the challenge to nurture and develop his talent. They conducted an informal assessment through an interview and found that Kevin already knew almost all the material that would normally be dealt with in the ninth-grade general science course. He knew some of the material in the 10th-grade biology curriculum, but expressed keen interest in several of the topics in that area that were new to him. As a result, the team arranged to waive his enrollment in general science. They created some study materials and reading assignments to deal with selected topics that were unfamiliar to him and placed him in an honors section of the 10th-grade biology course as a freshman. In addition, Kevin was invited to join with several other students who had previously been successful in the science fair to explore possible topics for this year's projects.

What might we learn from this story? It illustrates many of the basic concepts and principles of Level III of the LoS approach in action: activities and services you can provide for some students on a consistent basis. In this chapter, we will guide you in carrying out Level III in your own classroom, school, or district.

What Are Level III Services?

Level III programming focuses on in-depth studies that provide a high level of challenge for a small number of students who are prepared and motivated for those experiences. Level III options are designed for individuals who demonstrate sustained competence, interest, and ability in any discipline or talent domain—options through which you recognize and respond to the student's emerging need for more extensive and varied experiences. We describe Level III as responding to the needs of students who are "Enthusiastic and Performing."

Screening and selection for participation in Level III opportunities relate directly to the needs that are evident in the students and the opportunities that link to them. The process uses specific information related to the activity to document student characteristics necessary for effective performance. For example, in selecting students to participate in a particular advanced mathematics or science program, planners choose criteria that relate directly to the students' skills, achievement, reasoning ability, motivation, and interest in the relevant areas of mathematics or science.

Program designers ensure that Level III options are substantially different from the regular curriculum. They define each Level III program option clearly in relation to its prerequisite skills, goals, objectives, and indicators of success. Level III opportunities often extend beyond the school day and can involve the students in regularly scheduled small-group or individual activities.

As in the previous two levels, Level III can involve the energy and efforts of staff, home, and community. However, at Level III, the objective is to tap into the skills and talents of those who will be able to provide advanced learning opportunities. These are individuals who not only possess a high degree of competence in their talent domain, but may have access to additional resources and experts.

Rationale and Purposes

Why do we include Level III in our approach to programming for talent development? What purposes do Level III services have in relation to our overall goals for programming?

- **Focus on Individual Strengths and Talents.** At Level III, programming opportunities and services shift from a general focus aimed at groups of students to a focus aimed specifically at the unique strengths and talents of individuals. While all students participate in Level I activities and many students participate in a variety of different Level II opportunities, participation by students in Level III services is selective, and so we describe Level III as for "some" students. It is based on data (some of which may be gathered during Level I and Level II activities) that document and demonstrate a student's sustained interests, strengths, and talents—her or his "positive needs" as a learner.

- **Responds to the Positive Needs of Students.** Some students have programmatic needs that arise from their strengths and talent potentials. Students who should be engaged in Level III services need high-level educational opportunities and experiences that are appropriate, challenging, and developmental. These students are ready for more challenging, higher level, rigorous learning in the area or areas of their strengths and talents. Level III activities also provide opportunities for students to apply creative thinking, critical thinking, and problem-solving skills and tools to complex problems and challenges, using their process expertise in powerful ways. Level III services respond in appropriate ways to those who strive to demonstrate and apply their talents in increasingly complex ways. Level III is about getting them on the "fast track" toward becoming experts in their field of interest and nurturing their emerging passion.

- **Affirming the Students' Awareness of Their Talents.** Level III services affirm the value of students' motivation and hard work as they expand and extend their interests and talents. The message you convey to these potential candidates is, "You are doing something great. Let us help you to become more proficient in the area you have chosen." It is about honoring and stretching students' growing awareness of their emerging passion for an area of interest.

Implementing Level III Services for Some Students

There are four important "keys to success" in implementing Level III programming. They deal with continuing to build on what is already known about students and offering programming designed to respond to their strengths and sustained interests. The keys involve a team approach in which classroom teachers, support staff, administrators, students, and parents can participate collaboratively in designing and implementing appropriate and challenging programming opportunities for students. Figure 15 summarizes the four keys to success for Level III.

Keys to Success in LoS Programming: Level III

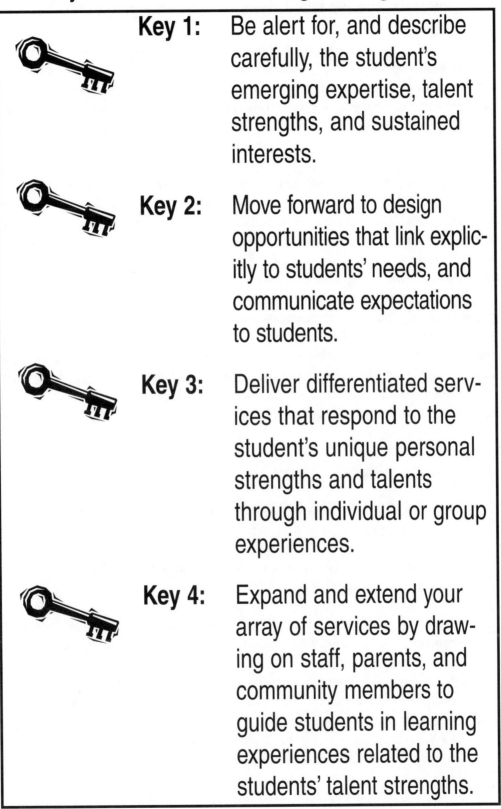

Key 1: Be alert for, and describe carefully, the student's emerging expertise, talent strengths, and sustained interests.

Key 2: Move forward to design opportunities that link explicitly to students' needs, and communicate expectations to students.

Key 3: Deliver differentiated services that respond to the student's unique personal strengths and talents through individual or group experiences.

Key 4: Expand and extend your array of services by drawing on staff, parents, and community members to guide students in learning experiences related to the students' talent strengths.

Figure 15: Keys to Success for Level III

Key 1: Be alert for, and describe carefully, an individual's sustained interests, specific talent strengths, and emerging expertise.

This key deals with the ways in which you determine and document student needs and individual strengths that call for significant differentiation of instruction. Talents are sometimes overlooked because teachers typically don't think of themselves as talent spotters. Keep in mind that what you (and many others in the student's life) do everyday counts. Level III involves active talent spotting to gain an awareness of students' emerging expertise. It is about a commitment to serve individualized strengths and talents.

Unlike the open, invitational nature of Levels I and II, Level III involves specific criteria for participation in the activities or services. Documenting student needs is a diagnostic process that is concerned with extending the student's strengths and talents. It is not simply determining whether or not the student should be included in (or excluded from) a certain category. In Level III, there is an emphasis on "goodness of fit," in which students have access to services that are appropriate and challenging. The selection criteria are not concerned with "eligibility" as much as they are with stating clearly the skills or competencies essential for successful engagement. To document a student's Level III needs, it is important to look for ways to use a variety of student information, many parts of which may be readily available. For example, a student who has straight As in science and a statewide science fair award demonstrates an obvious need for extended enrichment programming in science. In Level III, describing the student's needs involves:

- Acting as a "talent spotter," a person who actively looks for students' strengths, talents, and interests.

- Training staff in assessment practices and how to recognize personal characteristics of advanced students.

- Considering students' performance history and products indicating successful experience and participation in related or background areas.

- Analyzing both formal and informal information about students to build profiles of students' learning characteristics and programming needs.

- Accepting referrals or nominations by others, including the student's own expressed interest in Level III services.

- Considering many cumulative sources of data such as teachers, parents, and students that is updated and passed on from year to year.

- Listening to students and parents to learn about activities and interests that take place outside the school setting.

- Talking with and listening to students in order to understand their unique characteristics and needs.

- Recognizing and honoring varied strengths, talents, and learning styles.

- Being attentive and responsive to students' economic conditions, gender, developmental differences, handicapping conditions, and other factors that might mitigate against fair assessment practices.

Key 2: Move forward to design opportunities that link explicitly with the student's needs and communicate expectations clearly.

This key deals with the ways in which you define, develop, and share criteria for successful participation in specific Level III opportunities. When you offer a student the opportunity to participate in Level III services, you must let the student know what is at stake. After an initial feeling of pride, some students may wonder if they are up to the challenge or even if they want to accept the challenge. Ensure that you have a match between the student's needs and his or her commitment by delineating expectations in clear and concise language. Candidates must be able to discern the type and quality of work, time requirements, schedule of activities, and indicators of success that will be expected of them. In Level III, designing opportunities and communicating expectations that link with student needs involves:

- Providing scheduled time and support for staff to work together to review and discuss the positive needs of students (strengths, interests, and characteristics).

- Consistently following specific procedures for collecting data used in developing talent profiles that document student needs.

- Maintaining an appropriate balance of quantitative and qualitative measures with adequate evidence of reliability and validity throughout the profiling process.

- Planning appropriate and challenging responses to demonstrated and documented student needs.

- Implementing specific action plans that clearly describe and set forth the specific challenges and requirements of each Level III opportunity.

- Clearly defining the characteristics of students and prerequisite skills that provide a foundation for sustained involvement and acquisition of expertise in each Level III opportunity.

- Communicating information explicitly to staff, students, and parents about expectations for various Level III activities.

Key 3: Deliver differentiated services that respond to the student's unique personal strengths and talents through individual or group experiences.

This key deals with the ways in which you differentiate Level III activities from the regular curriculum. Level III services are designed to respond to the unmet needs of students we describe as "enthusiastic performers." Students who demonstrate advanced talent and interest need opportunities to develop their expertise and passion by working at higher levels of intellectual demand. Based on their interests and learning preferences, they are ready to apply their strengths in personal ways. Some Level III activities, for example, include honors classes, advanced or AP (Advanced Placement) courses, seminars or advanced electives in specific content or talent areas, group problem-solving challenges or projects, or participation in groups in which membership involves an audition or demonstration of accomplishments in a particular talent area.

You offer a Level III service when there is evidence of the need for that particular opportunity; it is not necessarily a programming feature that is *always* offered. If, at a particular time, no students need a specific service, then it would not be offered. On the other hand, if there are students with unmet needs and the appropriate services do not exist, it is important to create or schedule those services in response to the identified needs. In Level III, delivering differentiated services involves:

- Training staff about differentiating the curriculum to respond to students' unique strengths and talents.

- Involving students in high levels of creative and critical thinking as well as metacognition, when addressing complex issues and dilemmas.

- Providing contexts that are authentic, meaningful, and mentally inviting to students in which they can apply thinking tools and skills to realistic and real-life challenges.

- Promoting understanding, rather than rote learning, and dealing with complex and ambiguous issues.

- Focusing on in-depth studies that provide a high level of challenge for a small number of students.

- Challenging the student's developing competence into a commitment to creative production.

- Helping students to move toward expert levels of performance by guiding them to encounter and embrace high-level challenges.

- Guiding students in mastering key information, ideas, and skills to promote understanding of their talent area.

- Maintaining rigorous standards by making clear the students' responsibility to exhibit a high level of commitment and self-direction.

- Engaging students in goal setting consistent with personal aspirations and interests to help them acquire confidence, courage, and a sense of self, despite obstacles that they might encounter.

- Challenging students' developing competence into a commitment to exercise independence in thought and behavior as creative producers.

- Focusing on in-depth studies and ensuring an appropriate level and pace of instruction to match students' abilities.

Key 4: Expand and extend your array of services by drawing on staff, parents, and community members to guide students in learning experiences related to the students' talent strengths.

This key deals with the ways in which you locate and match additional resources with students who need Level III opportunities. Level III services link students with specialists from the school, home, and community. Every community is rich in diversely talented people. These are individuals who may have pursued their own interests as hobbies, as volunteers, or in their careers. Most would be willing to assume some role in Level III services, provided that the roles are well defined. Level III also provides an opportunity for students to offer their talents in service to the community. Use your daily contacts to help build a list of resources. In Level III, stretching delivery of services involves:

- Training staff about team building and action planning.

- Creating "curriculum enhancement" teams (include representatives from home, school, and community) to stimulate innovation. These teams can explore creative ways to locate and link resources (people, places, and things) with student needs.

- Creating and drawing on a "community resource pool."

- Developing opportunities for mentoring and role modeling in talent and career areas.

- Forming partnerships with community agencies and organizations.

- Encouraging and supporting programming that crosses age, grade, or building lines.

- Helping students learn how to gain access to resources (people, things, and places).

- Linking classroom learning with out-of-school events, places, materials, and people.

- Exploring together (staff, students, parents) how to provide resources (materials and lessons) to support and develop a student's talent.

- Promoting community awareness of the LoS approach and its benefits.

- Creating learning environments for students that allow for interactions and collaboration with others that respect diversity, and encourage flexible thinking and social competence.

Some initial steps in implementing Level III might be to examine your current programming practices in relation to the four keys. Make a list of all the services that are relevant for Level III. Identify which students have unique strengths and interests. Convene a building-level planning team to analyze the needs of students and explore appropriate Level III responses.

Illustrative Examples of Level III Services

As with the previous two levels, specific Level III services will vary in any class, school, or district. We will not attempt to provide a single, fixed set of "official" Level III services in this section. We will, however, provide several specific illustrative examples of Level III services organized around the four keys. These examples are drawn from our experiences in working with teachers and schools using the LoS approach.

Key 1: Be alert for, and describe carefully, an individual's sustained interests, specific talent strengths, and emerging expertise.

Example: In an elementary school, teachers surveyed students about their interests and activities through a questionnaire. They gathered information about areas the students were involved in outside of school and were able to use that information in creating differentiated curricular opportunities based on unique interests for small groups of students.

Example: A middle school teacher discovered through a casual conversation with a student that he had an interest in and experience with bow and arrow making. This conversation led to a number of interesting and challenging curricular opportunities for the student. One in particular involved the student in making a presentation to a group of elementary students who were studying about Native Americans.

Example: Middle and high school band students prepared for and participated in regional solo and ensemble competitions. Music professionals rated their performances and technical proficiency and gave them constructive feedback to help them improve.

Example: There are many levels of involvement available in athletics based on interest and performance. All students might participate in sports, but only some are involved at the varsity level.

Example: After attending an in-service workshop on authentic assessment, a high school math teacher initiated performance assessment panels for semester exams. He assigned challenging problems to groups of students. They prepared detailed solutions that they presented to the assessment panels. The teacher and gifted specialist recruited panel members from the community, the school district, the local community college faculty and students, and the local university faculty and students. The panels used a rubric developed by the teacher with assistance from the gifted specialist to rate the individual student performances. Each panel member provided specific written feedback to support their ratings.

Example: The staff in an elementary school had an in-service on assessing creativity characteristics. The teachers, with assistance from their gifted programming specialist, developed and used a variety of checklists that helped them to observe and document specific personal creativity characteristics among their students. For example, they looked for students who demonstrated specific characteristics associated with generating ideas during a brainstorming session.

Example: In one school district, the gifted staff reviewed test questions and related materials to avoid potentially insensitive content and language. They selected and used tests that were as fair as possible for all test takers. They also looked beyond test scores to find evidence of talent by including sources of data other than tests, such as portfolios, interest inventories, and rating scales completed by parents and peers.

Key 2: Move forward to design opportunities that link explicitly with the student's needs and to communicate expectations clearly.

Example: Middle school teachers used some of their team planning time to discuss with the guidance counselor and gifted specialist the results of the annual talent search program. Seventh-grade students scoring at or above the 95th percentile on a standardized test in mathematics or verbal areas were eligible to participate in the program. They took the Scholastic Aptitude Test designed for college-bound high school juniors.

Example: In a high school, the science department staff and guidance counselors met during weekly scheduled department planning time to review the results of the annual statewide test for academic standards. They looked for students who showed mastery in science and then actively worked to enroll those students in appropriate courses.

Example: A high school chemistry teacher reviewed the objectives and format for his Advanced Placement course and established criteria for successful participation in the course. The teacher communicated the criteria to prospective students to help them make informed decisions about participating.

Example. The staff of an elementary school met in grade-level and content-areas planning teams on a regular basis. They reviewed their students' work in several core content areas and identified small clusters of students who would benefit from advanced work in one or more areas. They monitored the students' progress throughout the year and adjusted the groups as warranted. The teachers also developed plans for cross-age or multiage groups when appropriate for meeting students' needs.

Example: In conjunction with the People to People program, sixth- and seventh-grade students are nominated by teachers, guidance counselors, or community leaders to be "student ambassadors" to foreign countries. They spend 3 weeks sightseeing and living with families in a host country.

Example: A high school staff developed an Advanced Placement course catalogue that described the courses and criteria for successful participation in each course. They mailed a copy to each household in the school's attendance area. The counselors presented a booklet to each student during their annual course planning meeting.

Key 3: Deliver differentiated services that respond to the student's unique personal strengths and talents through individual or group experiences.

Example: The gifted programming specialist conducted a workshop for an elementary school staff on curriculum compacting. Teachers pretested their students before beginning a unit of instruction. Students with at least 95% mastery were given alternative assignments based on their interests in that content area.

Example: In a middle school, the gifted programming specialist met with small groups of students to investigate real problems. One group was concerned about traffic congestion in front of the school at the end of the day. They worked on improving the traffic flow for cars, busses, and pedestrians. They generated ideas, focused on a promising solution, and created an action plan that was implemented by the school administration.

Example: A high school offered seminars during study hall periods as an option for interested students. Guest speakers from a variety of fields (the arts, academia, business, technology, etc.) conducted these seminars.

Example: A gifted programming specialist met with fifth-grade students to teach them about personal problem solving. They identified areas of personal strength and interest. Then, they established some short- and long-term goals in those areas. In their planning, they considered possible obstacles and barriers to reaching their goals. They turned them into positive challenges by considering ways to overcome these possible limitations.

Example: A high school offered Advanced Placement courses in which students studied college-level material and prepared to take Advanced Placement exams in order to earn college credit.

Example: In a first-grade classroom, a parent worked with several children interested in architecture to create drawings and models of futuristic buildings.

Key 4: Expand and extend your array of services by drawing on staff, parents, and community members to guide students in learning experiences related to the students' talent strengths.

Example: Staff in an elementary school attended a half-day workshop on problem-solving styles. They learned about the different ways people manage change and approach problems. They each took VIEW: An Assessment of Problem Solving Style online before the workshop. At the workshop, they received their individual reports and learned about the different styles among the staff. They used this information to help better understand their own strengths, the strengths of others, and the different styles among students.

Example: A group of middle school students in an advanced science class participated in the Jason Project through the local science museum. The students became part of a live underwater science research project through an interactive distance learning connection with the Jason explorers.

Example: Students in grades 3–5 shared a common interest in inventing. They met and worked on activities together once a week under the direction of the gifted programming specialist. Despite the differences in age, students had much in common, and friendships developed across grade levels.

Example: In a regional area, special interest performance groups such as jazz bands, symphony orchestras, drama clubs, choral groups, and dance ensembles were composed of students from several school buildings and districts. They practiced once a week after school and gave four public performances during the school year.

Example: A group of talented high school band students formed a jazz group that performed at community events.

Example: A school district sponsored competitive programs such as Science Olympiad, Future Problem Solving, and Destination ImagiNation®. Students met to practice after school with volunteer coaches (teachers and parents) and attended the annual regional competition.

Example: A middle school Destination ImagiNation® team competed at the regional level and qualified for the state finals.

Example: Students in grade 6 who tested at grade level 9 or higher on a reading test in vocabulary and comprehension participated in a Junior Great Books discussion group. A parent who became a trained facilitator met with them once a week during language arts class.

Example: The local gifted programming specialist made a presentation at a PTA meeting to explain the school's LoS program and to enlist volunteers.

Example: Students were recognized for their accomplishments by the local Kiwanis Club at one of their regular meetings.

The Rest of the Story ...

Kevin completed the supplementary assignments from the general science curriculum promptly and at a very high level of quality. Based on the work he did in those assignments, he asked several questions that surprised the science teacher because of the insight and grasp of the concepts in the responses. This led to some additional suggestions for reading, which Kevin pursued eagerly and then discussed with the teacher. Kevin also continued to do outstanding work in the biology class throughout the year.

Later in the year, Mrs. Lightjohn, the chair of the science department, invited Kevin and his parents to meet with her, two of the science teachers, and a gifted programming specialist to begin planning for his next steps in the school's science program. The Martels listened attentively as the teachers gave them an overview of their talent development program. West High's program, they said, was student-driven. It was based on the dis-

trict's philosophy that all teachers must be on the lookout for student talent. They held the belief that all students at all grade levels deserved to have opportunities to demonstrate their talents and sustained interests. When individuals emerged with obvious strengths, the teachers' challenge was to find ways to develop their individual talents. This led to a discussion of a number of future possibilities that Kevin found very exciting. The school required all students to engage in several hours of community service each year, and the gifted and talented program specialist arranged for several students to volunteer in community agencies related to their interests and talents. Kevin expressed a keen interest in volunteering at the local science museum.

LoS Level III Planning Guide

Use the Planning Guides in Figures 16 and 17 to assist you in planning Level III activities for your school or district. Many schools have found these guides valuable for discussion and planning purposes. For example, you might ask each person to prepare their own forms, then discuss them in grade-level groups, and then to consider them again in relation to content, process, and product differentiation that takes place in your school.

What Level III activities do we now offer for students who are capable of advanced applications of thinking processes?	What Level III activities do we now offer for students who need opportunities for advanced work in specific content areas?
What opportunities do students have to provide service to the school or the community?	What advanced product or performance opportunities do we offer our students?

Figure 16: Identifying Present Level III Activities

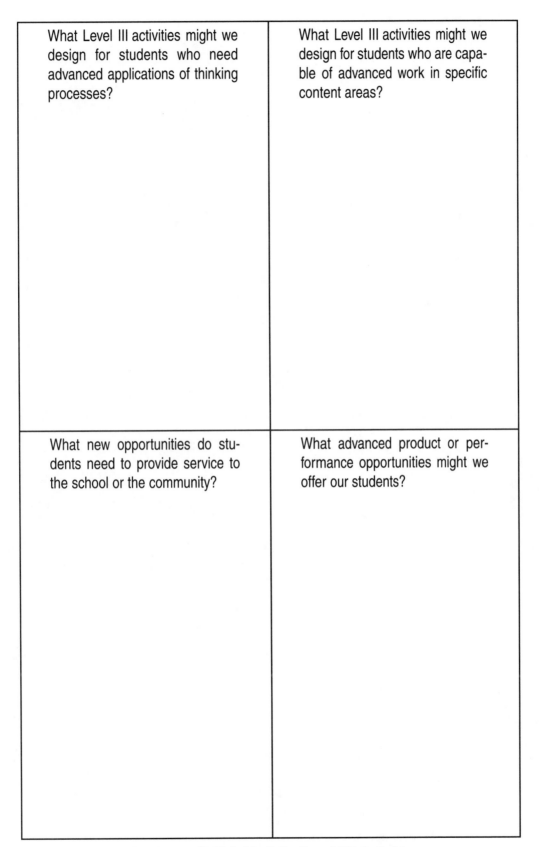

What Level III activities might we design for students who need advanced applications of thinking processes?	What Level III activities might we design for students who are capable of advanced work in specific content areas?
What new opportunities do students need to provide service to the school or the community?	What advanced product or performance opportunities might we offer our students?

Figure 17: "Wish List" for Level III Activities

Chapter 6
Level IV: Programming for a Few Students

This chapter begins with an illustrative story. We then provide a brief description of Level IV services followed by our rationale and purposes for including them in the LoS approach to talent development. Next, we present three important "keys to success" in implementing Level IV programming. We also offer illustrations and examples of Level IV in action and provide examples of Level IV services in various settings, content areas, and grade levels.

Sarah's Independent Research Project

Sarah, a second-grade student, was performing far beyond all the other students in her class in most situations from day to day. As a result, her classroom teacher turned to Ms. White, the gifted programming specialist (GPS) at school, for additional ideas and support. The teacher had documented Sarah's superior reading ability and knew she needed additional opportunities beyond the teacher's highest reading group to explore her talents and interests. Sarah was already working on a variety of activities and assignments well beyond those of other students in the classroom. She already worked with a small group of advanced readers from grades 4–5 on a regular basis. Even with the teacher's active efforts to differentiate instruction for Sarah, it was clear that she needed more complex learning challenges. Through discussions with the classroom teacher and with Sarah, Ms. White discovered that Sarah was very interested in the Pan American Exposition of 1901. Her family had several treasured souvenirs from the Exposition, and her great-grandfather, who had visited the Exposition as a young boy and was still living, often recalled his experiences there with great excitement.

Ms. White suggested that Sarah begin her personal investigation of this event by documenting her great-grandfather's recollections of his visits to the Exposition. Sarah's mother arranged for both Sarah and Ms. White to visit the great-grandfather. Ms. White took pictures and audiotaped Sarah's conversation with her great-grandfather. Using the souvenirs and pictures, he talked about the Electric Light Tower, his visits to the midway, and meeting the Native American chief Geronimo.

Ms. White arranged a special field trip for Sarah, which included visits to the Buffalo and Erie County Historical Society (the only remaining permanent building from the Exposition), historical markers where President William McKinley was shot, the location of the house where he died, and the Theodore Roosevelt Inaugural Site.

Over the next 2 years, Sarah met regularly with Ms. White to discuss her project. Ms. White looked for community resources that would be of interest to Sarah. The Theodore Roosevelt Inaugural Site held a Victorian Camp during the summer, which proved very useful and so Sarah attended it twice. She learned what life was like for youngsters during that time, including games children played, the clothes they wore, the food they ate, and how they traveled.

Sarah's parents arranged for follow-up visits with her great-grandfather and additional trips to the local library and the Historical Society library, where she was able to use many primary sources. She documented her experiences through pictures and collected information in a journal.

What might you learn from this story? It illustrates many of the basic concepts and principles of Level IV in the LoS approach in action—activities and services you can provide for a few students. In this chapter, we will guide you in carrying out Level IV in your own classroom, school, or district.

What Are Level IV Services?

Level IV in the LoS approach focuses on responding to the unique strengths and needs of a few students whose talents far outstrip the school's customary curricular and instructional program. We describe this level as "soaring and passionate" to reflect the blossoming expertise of students who receive Level IV services. Their documented strengths, talents, interests, and potentials require a customized or individually designed response. Such experiences are "one of a kind" and tailored to the student's personal profile of demonstrated and sustained strengths. Level IV services are carefully planned and based on a detailed review of all available data. Efforts to document the student's exceptional needs and strengths often include conferences with the student, with other teachers who know the student's work and accomplishments well, with leaders of programs outside the school in which the student may be involved, and with the student's parents.

Level IV activities are advanced and challenging. Their content emphasizes productive thinking and original inquiry within any talent area or domain. Level IV services represent unique work or projects that involve rigorous content, processes, or products and exceed the activities or expectations normally held for students of similar chronological age. They ordinarily involve independent, original work that leads to an authentic product or performance that is credible in relation to the expectations, standards, and practices of professionals within that talent domain.

Level IV programming addresses the *content, process, affective,* and *product* dimensions of the student's talent development.

In relation to *content*, Level IV activities provide high-level, complex, challenging curricula, including a variety of accelerative options and strategies. For example, a student might complete 2 years of algebra in a special program that only meets one afternoon per week or in a 4-week summer program. Level IV services can include early admission or early graduation, dual enrollment, grade advancement, accelerated content provided for younger students in their core grade placement (e.g., enabling a student in grade 2 to pursue work at the fifth- or sixth-grade level within a grade 2 classroom), or advanced private lessons. It can also include opportunities to "test out" of courses or specific course requirements or options such as credit by examination or various kinds of distance learning (e.g., correspondence courses or online programs).

In the *process* dimension, Level IV activities engage students in first-hand research and inquiry, creativity, and the search for solutions to complex problems and challenges in the school, community, or specific content or talent area. Level IV services also focus on the development and use of metacognitive skills in real-life situations (monitoring, managing, and modifying processes while working on the tasks).

The *affective* dimension of Level IV emphasizes self-management and self-development. Level IV services help students to find and construct future pathways and develop their personal commitment within the talent area. Students grow into the role of an expert practitioner and enjoy the autonomy of personal talent by learning the behavioral, social, and performance norms of that area.

The *product* dimension involves opportunities to share authentic products with real outlets and audiences. Students who are involved in Level IV services may attain recognition and support for the projects and products in a variety of ways, including publications, advanced academic credit or standing, obtaining a patent, writing or obtaining grants to support their projects, selection for highly competitive programs or performance groups, or involvement in activities of outside organizations or events.

Level IV services relate specifically to an individual student's advanced skills and abilities (revealed through performance or test data, or both), strong and sustained interests, and, in many cases, documentation of previous experience and outstanding performance or exceptionally strong passion for a topic or talent domain. They are services that are vital and valid parts of their overall school experience, and they extend beyond being enjoyable clubs or after-school activities. They involve deep and sustained engagement in learning experiences that tap the passion of the student's talents, skills, and aspirations.

Level IV involves designing individual plans and challenging new opportunities that will enable the student to progress in significant and original directions within the talent area and to pursue projects or activities that emphasize creative productivity. These services emphasize what the student designs, does, and documents, and so extends significantly beyond routine, prescribed assignments, activities, or exercises in a course or basic curriculum. In a classroom context, they involve rigorous and complex content, strong creative and critical thinking applications, and high expectations for quality of work. In addition to advanced course content, however, Level IV services extend into the real world of the professional in a talent domain in a way that is appropriate in relation to the student's development, maturity, and experience.

In summary, Level IV provides a context that "sets the bar high" in content, allows students "freedom to act" on ideas and topics based on their personal interests, and engages them in creating original products to share with authentic audiences and to solve real problems creatively.

Rationale and Purposes

In this section, we will consider the rationale for Level IV in the LoS framework and the unique and important purposes that Level IV services serve in relation to our overall goals for programming.

- **Responsive to Unique Individual Strengths, Talents, and Interests.** Level IV services are individually planned responses to a student's outstanding and sustained strengths, talents, and interests. Each plan is based on a profile of information collected about the student. The profile of a student who needs Level IV services generally indicates a "track record" of preparation or readiness for highly advanced and intense engagement in a talent area. It is often the case that the student who needs Level IV services is so obvious to everyone who knows her or him that it is more difficult, and perhaps less accurate and effective, for us to describe that instance in technical terms than it is simply to say, "You'll know when Level IV services are appropriate when you meet the student who needs them!" (A wag once referred to this as "interocular significance," or so obviously important that "it hits you between the eyes.") The challenge of responding to a student's individual needs is complicated and demanding and sometimes requires setting aside general rules and procedures or granting permission to make exceptions based on extraordinary cases. However, recognizing and responding to a student's exceptional strengths and talents, nurturing the student's passion to excel in an area, and serving as a catalyst for "blossoming expertise" is one of the most powerful and rewarding challenges in education.

- **Responds to the Need for High-level Content Challenge.** Level IV services build on the knowledge and conceptual base of a talent area or domain. A student who needs Level IV services has the ability, the preparation, and the motivation to engage in, comprehend, and organize rigorous, complex content, to master challenging concepts, principles, and relationships, and to analyze and evaluate that material. Level IV services respond to the needs of students who "hunger and thirst" for knowledge in domains or topic areas that capture their interest over a sustained period of time. They may be voracious in their quest for new ideas and information about their passions, and they often demonstrate an encyclopedic knowledge, constant curiosity, and boundless enthusiasm for sharing their knowledge. Programming that includes effective acceleration helps to maximize the development of strengths and talents by providing instruction at appropriate rate and pace based on the student's characteristics and abilities. It involves ensuring that students spend only the amount of time they need to master lessons. It provides freedom from boredom and unnecessary repetition or instruction. It includes radical forms of acceleration such as multiple grade advancement, early entrance, dual enrollments, distance learning, or early graduation.

- **Responds to the Need for High-level Process Challenge.** The high level of challenge associated with Level IV services includes content mastery, but it extends beyond content alone and involves many other challenging dimensions. A high level of challenge in one's expertise or talent area also involves the challenge to learn and apply powerful process tools and strategies used by practicing professionals in real life. These include methods for research and inquiry, creative and critical thinking, problem solving, and change management and applying those methods to real-life opportunities and challenges. (Many of these process skills and tools may have been learned through other LoS activities and services and are now being applied at a higher level and for more complex tasks.) Level IV process involvement creates challenges for students not just to learn about, but also to learn how and when, to learn to improve what exists, and to extend learning in new directions. Creative challenges in any situation require sustained time and effort, and Level IV prepares students for those endeavors.

- **Builds Expertise and Productivity as a Professional in a Talent Domain.** Acquiring competence in relevant, useful content in one's area of expertise ignites and sustains passions for that talent domain. Functioning as a producer and a potential scholar in an area serves as a catalyst for self-definition and self-understanding. Assuming the role of a professional allows the student to reflect on the impact of the area on the self and the lives of others in the wider world. Programming helps students to acquire the accumulated and shared wisdom, culture, values, expectations, and norms associated with the talent area. It offers students an opportunity for recognition and acceptance of their independence and evolving maturity.

Implementing Level IV Services for a Few Students

There are three important "keys to success" in implementing Level IV programming. These are summarized in Figure 18.

Keys to Success in LoS Programming: Level IV

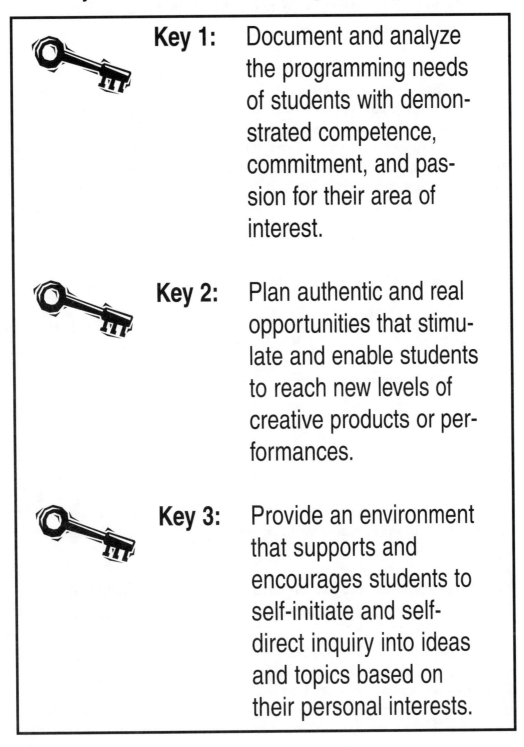

Key 1: Document and analyze the programming needs of students with demonstrated competence, commitment, and passion for their area of interest.

Key 2: Plan authentic and real opportunities that stimulate and enable students to reach new levels of creative products or performances.

Key 3: Provide an environment that supports and encourages students to self-initiate and self-direct inquiry into ideas and topics based on their personal interests.

Figure 18: Keys to Success for Level IV

Key 1: Document and analyze the programming needs of students with demonstrated competence, commitment, and passion for their area of interest.

This key deals with the ways in which you determine the nature and depth of a student's commitment and strengths in a specific area of interest. In Level IV, your role is completing the transition from talent spotter to talent developer that has emerged through the four levels. You can expect to find new and different situations. You begin by asking questions such as, "What is the student's track record of preparation and readiness for a highly individualized experience? What evidence is there to indicate sustained personal interest, intrinsic motivation, and passion for the area?" In Level IV, documenting and analyzing the programming needs of students involves:

- Clarifying responsibilities of the student, the school, and the parents.

- Knowing and understanding personal creativity characteristics.

- Knowing and understanding a variety of instruments and techniques for assessing achievement, abilities, and style preferences.

- Understanding how to interpret test scores.

- Using fair and appropriate assessment procedures.

- Recognizing how a student may be a "trend setter" or how he or she influences others through "contagious enthusiasm" in the area of interest.

- Understanding what makes the student a "resident expert" at something in the school and how that might be respected by other students and teachers (or might not!).

Key 2: Plan authentic and real opportunities that stimulate and enable students to reach new levels of creative products or performances.

This key involves the ways in which you help students learn how to analyze, evaluate, and make decisions about ideas and how to discover and approach problems. Preparing your students of today for the challenges of tomorrow requires helping them to accept and manage change constructively. By applying a problem-solving approach and some inventive thinking, you can help them to grow in expertise and creatively productive accomplishments. Creating original products requires some comfort with the unknown; an ability to recognize problems where they exist, often before others become aware of them, and the desire to both analyze and play with problems and possible solutions. Acquisition of expert knowledge demands investment of considerable effort and persistence over time. Tasks must be interesting and personally relevant to facilitate intrinsic motivation. As students move into areas of their passion, they want to participate in decision making, and they can be involved quite effectively in planning and carrying out many aspects of their own learning. The teacher's role is to delegate many of the process decisions and actions to the students, but also to be there to answer questions, to cut through the red tape, and to support them as they struggle through inevitable bumps in the road, and, finally to celebrate their successes. In Level IV, planning authentic opportunities involves:

- Providing opportunities individually or in small groups to investigate real problems and to conduct firsthand investigations that lead to original products.

- Communicating and celebrating (i.e., share, present, display, publish) their products and accomplishments with appropriate outlets.

- Providing access to many and varied resources, including materials and people throughout the community or on a broader basis through the Internet.

- Facilitating access to and support for programs and events outside the school setting.

- Helping students to understand the nature of change in our world and its personal and career implications for them.

- Initiating job shadowing, internships, and mentoring experiences.

- Involving students in developing rubrics for products that include expert-level indicators.

- Encouraging collaborations between students and adult experts.

- Helping students to translate their potential for independence into effective skills by giving them opportunities to manage and direct their own projects.

Key 3: Provide an environment that supports and encourages students to self-initiate and self-direct inquiry into ideas and topics based on their personal interests.

This key involves the ways in which you encourage students to be in charge of their own learning and stimulate creatively productive outcomes. Part of Level IV programming is resolving scheduling, credit issues, logistics, and other challenges faced by the school and the student. It is also about helping students to discover and create self. It includes developing a positive identity, a sense of purpose, and a positive view of their future.

Experiences necessary to acquire the discipline and work habits that lead to self-direction and lifelong learning involve setting goals, independently carrying out projects, and evaluating one's own work. High-level accomplishment requires self-discipline, persistence, and sustained involvement to gain expertise. An interactive and collaborative instructional context stimulates reflective thinking and enhances high-level learning. Students need to become confident and courageous in pursuing goals and purposes despite obstacles. Recognize that, when people say, "Gifted students need time and experiences with their peers," we hope they are really describing specific, targeted Level IV programming. In Level IV, providing an environment that supports self-direction involves:

- Giving credit for involvement in independent study, investigations of real problems, or studying advanced topics as an incentive to engage in them.

- Encouraging students to learn about famous people in their area of interest and the role of discipline in their success.

- Requiring personal goals and timelines for projects and tasks.

- Teaching students appropriate methods for locating their own materials and resources.

- Teaching students methods for realistic self-evaluation.

- Demonstrating a positive regard for learning, thinking, and inquiry.

- Providing opportunities to interact with others who share similar abilities and accomplishments in areas of common interest.

- Providing access to teachers, mentors, and materials for advanced study opportunities commensurate with their experience, skills, and interests at home and within the community.

- Providing experiences that invite students to discover, explore, or construct career possibilities or opportunities.

Illustrative Examples of Level IV Services

Level IV services are, by definition, unique responses to the talents and needs of specific students. Of course, then, there is no preset list or set of services for this section. We will, however, provide several specific illustrative examples of Level IV services arranged by the three keys. As in the previous levels, these examples are drawn from our experiences in working with teachers and schools using the LoS approach.

Key 1: Document and analyze the programming needs of students with demonstrated competence, commitment, and passion for their area of interest.

Example: A high school band teacher noted that one of his musicians was not performing up to her ability. In conversations with her and looking at her portfolio, it was apparent that she had ambitions to pursue a career involving her chosen instrument. He realized that the instrument she played was not appropriate for the marching band program, but very important to her and her parents. He suggested that she try out for the regional youth symphony orchestra. She was accepted into the program and soon was enthusiastic about her music again because she was receiving appropriate and challenging instruction.

Example: A preschool student attended the annual kindergarten round-up program to determine if he was ready to begin kindergarten in the fall. The staff discovered that he was already reading and possessed the readiness skills for first grade. It was decided to enroll him in first grade instead of kindergarten.

Example: A middle school student participated in a talent search program. His math scores on the SAT put him in the 95th percentile for college-bound seniors. He was placed in a regional math program at the local university where he competed 2 years of algebra in a class that met one afternoon per week during the school year.

Example: A high school student showed mastery on the statewide assessment test in science and was awarded the science credits required for graduation. She then enrolled in science classes at the local community college.

Example: A high school English teacher learned that a student created her own cartoon character and a book of stories. The teacher arranged for her to create a regular comic strip for the school newspaper based on this character.

Example: A fourth-grade student showed exceptional interest and knowledge in science. The student's teacher met with the LoS specialist to develop a plan for assessing the student's level of achievement. The teacher and student also completed a checklist of characteristics of students with special talents in science. The school arranged a planning meeting (involving the student, the parents, the LoS specialist, the teacher, and the school principal) to create a plan of action for responding to the student's science talent. They arranged for the student to participate in an eighth grade science class.

Key 2: Plan authentic and real opportunities that stimulate and enable students to reach new levels of creative products or performances.

Example: The noise level in the school cafeteria was a constant problem. None of the suggestions or options implemented in the past worked. Mr. Green, the gifted programming specialist, handed this challenge to a small group of his students. They decided that they needed to take a fresh and comprehensive look at this issue. They did this by using the Creative Problem Solving process. The group discovered that there were many unexplored facets to the noise factor. They proposed solutions to the major ones in a plan of action that involved the whole school.

Example: A fourth-grade boy had a special interest in baseball card collecting. He asked his teacher if he could organize a kids-only baseball card trading day. She contacted the gifted specialist, who helped him explore the idea and create an action plan. The student then implemented the plan and organized a successful kids-only baseball card show. The teachers were surprised to observe how intense the students who attended were. They even observed some new interests and strengths of some students that were not evident in their classroom behaviors.

Example: The newspapers in Bridgetown were filled with reporting about dissent at the high school. The controversy centered around the type and quality of elective courses. Morale at the school was at an all-time low. The student senate decided that something positive had to be done to stop the complaining and to address the issue. They approached the administration with a recommendation that they convene a group of student, parent, and teacher volunteers to study the problem and propose alternatives.

Example: A third-grade student wrote and produced an original puppet show. The student created the puppets and the set for the puppet theater, and then presented the show to several first-grade classes.

Example: A group of students in grades 3–5 produced a Friday afternoon student news program and presented it over the intraschool cable television station. The program went "on the air" throughout the school year and was received positively by students and staff alike.

Example: A group of high school students used creative problem solving to redesign the school's after-school clubs and activities.

Example: A middle school student participated in a veterinary medicine enrichment opportunity and now travels to a local veterinarian's office once a week to help do research.

Key 3: Provide an environment that supports and encourages students to self-initiate and self-direct inquiry into ideas and topics based on their personal interests.

Example: Kara loved to draw, doodle, and make funny squiggles. From this hobby, she developed an interest in cartooning. She devoured books on the subject and played with her favorite cartoon characters by cutting up the strips and mixing and matching the characters and themes. By the end of third grade, she had created her own cartoon characters and entertained her friends, schoolmates, and family with her own weekly series.

Example: A group of middle school students were concerned about the heavy use of saturated fats, especially in fast foods. They decided to learn all about the effects of saturated fat on the body. This led them to investigate the types of fat that two fast food chains used in their food preparation. Once this was done, they created a PowerPoint presentation to educate students about potential problems that might arise from having too much saturated fat in one's diet and by consuming too much fast food.

Example: Membership in the Jonas Salk Science Club is limited to students who excel in science and have expressed an interest in pursuing a career in medicine. The members determine the particular theme or topic they wish to explore. One year, they focused on the role of researcher. The gifted specialist worked out a plan for the students with the local teaching hospital. The plan was quite detailed and identified research projects, specific tasks related to each topic, and a specific time commitment.

Example: A fourth grader contacted the high school and community libraries to locate and use resources for a research project on Sherlock Holmes and detective work.

The Rest of the Story ...

Level IV involves services that respond to students' unique, high-level strengths and talents and to interests and passions among students that require careful planning, support that often reaches beyond the convenience of the school's structure and schedule, and authentic investment that may continue through an extended period of time.

Sarah's 2 years of work on her project culminated in a slide presentation to her fourth-grade classmates. The students then participated in several activities typical of 1901: rolling hoops, playing jacks, and quilling art. They were also able to take a closer look at the family's souvenirs. Sarah summarized several of her journal entries and created articles that were published in the children's page of the local newspaper.

More About Our Story From Chapter 5 ...

Our story in Chapter 5 dealt with Kevin Martel, an outstanding young science student who participated in a number of Level III activities. His school's faculty also realized that Kevin needed additional opportunities that extended beyond what they were already providing for him. At a planning meeting, the faculty told the Martels about several opportunities that might be open to Kevin. These included Advanced Placement courses, community partnerships, competitions, club membership, and individualized projects or performances. Each program option was clearly defined and included specific expectations and criteria for admitting students. The criteria were based on the kinds of things the students must know and do to succeed in those options. The school followed specific procedures consistently for collecting data to assure that the options were properly matched to student needs. Students who were candidates for any of these options and chose to accept the challenge were advised that they would be responsible for exhibiting a high level of commitment and self-direction.

Kevin was more than ready to involve himself in the process, and his enthusiasm continued to soar after the meeting. It carried over into a conversation with Dr. Haas, the science museum director, in which he gave him a detailed account of his work. Kevin could not believe that the teachers wanted to know more about him and his special interests. He was concerned that he probably talked too much about his passion for science.

As Dr. Haas thought about his remarkable conversation with Kevin, he made a mental note to call Mrs. Lightjohn. Wouldn't it be great if they could design a program with Kevin to expand his contributions to the museum?

Eventually, Kevin's passion for science and his previous community service volunteer work at the science museum paved the way for him to pursue his interests and talents at a higher level. He designed three hands-on centers for youngsters and trained several volunteers to oversee the activities. Kevin's centers were a big hit with young children, as well as their parents. A letter in his file from Dr. Haas commended him for volunteer work.

LoS Level IV Planning Guide

Our Level IV Planning Guide in Figure 19 will help you to think about what kinds of responses you can and do make, or what responses you may need to prepare to make, to provide appropriate and challenging Level IV activities and services for students who need them.

When you see a student with highly unusual needs and outstanding talent in any of these areas ...	What Level IV responses would you be ready to make?
Mathematics	
Science	
Technology/Computers	
Fine Arts/Performing Arts	
Social/Behavioral Sciences	
Language, Literature, Writing	
Leadership, Interpersonal	

Figure 19: Level IV Planning Guide

Chapter 7
Planning for, Implementing, and Evaluating the LoS Approach

Successful implementation of the LoS approach does not "just happen" as if by a stroke of magic in any classroom, school, or school district. It requires careful planning, deliberate effort, and on-going evaluation. After presenting an initial story, we will address these important concerns in this concluding chapter.

The Lakeside Community Schools

The Lakeside Community School District has been involved in LoS programming for several years. Looking back at their experiences may help others to plan, implement, and evaluate their efforts effectively.

Lakeside CSD began by establishing a districtwide planning committee with staff, parent, and community participation. The committee reviewed and studied literature on gifted education, communicated with a number of experts in the field, attended conferences, and visited several other area school districts' programs. They decided to implement the LoS approach. Guided by a systematic planning model, they developed a district master plan with linkages to their existing school improvement and management plans. The committee also arranged opportunities for the proposed master plan to be reviewed and discussed by staff and parents in each school and with school board members. The district's professional development staff worked with the committee to design and implement a week-long staff development "academy" for teams from each school and a plan for on-going in-service based on the results of needs assessment surveys at each school. They also conducted specific programs for school board members, district- and building-level administrators, and parents.

Each school developed its own building action plan to guide implementation of LoS. The board of education adopted and funded a plan for LoS programming specialists (experienced teachers with training in LoS) to be appointed on a full-time basis, each serving two buildings in the district. These specialists worked closely with the staff in their schools in implementing LoS. They planned and prepared a variety of activities at various levels, conferred with and supported classroom teachers in classroom-based pro-

gramming, provided direct instruction (with an emphasis on thinking skills and processes), facilitated services by outside resource people and groups, and met together regularly as a group to coordinate district-level initiatives.

After an initial 3-year "start-up" period, the district worked with a team from an area university to design and conduct an evaluation of its LoS programming efforts and its impact.

The Lakeside story illustrates several important factors that contribute to implementing the LoS approach successfully in practical settings. This chapter will highlight several factors that contribute to success in applying LoS in practice.

A Systematic Approach to Planning

In our work with schools and school districts, we have found it helpful to use a systematic approach to planning, both for districts just beginning to create programming and for districts with a commitment to making a transition from more traditional program models to the LoS approach. There are many planning models for educational programs, but we have found that the six-stage process model illustrated in Figure 20 represents a practical and useful model that schools or districts can implement efficiently.

1. **Prepare**	2. **Clarify where you are now**
• Becoming aware of the importance, benefits, and the need for action • Gathering information • Understanding the philosophy, rationale, goals, and definitions • Making an informed commitment	• Finding present positives • Doing needs assessment • Considering your "wish list" • Checking the culture or climate for talent development

6. **Ensure quality, Innovation, & Continuous Improvement**	3. **Decide where to go next**
• Evaluating your efforts • Monitoring your progress • Being open to innovation • Practicing continuous improvement • Engaging in professional development	• Setting goals: maintaining positives • Setting goals: meeting needs or attaining the "wish list" • Current reality vs. desired future • Enlisting support, planning action • Create master plan, building plans

5. **Seek talents and strengths**	4. **Carry out programming**
• "Talent spotting" • Looking for strengths, talents, and interests in all students • Profiling for effective programming • Searching for helpful data (on-going)	Implementing: • In the regular classroom • In school—in addition to the regular classroom • In the home and community

Figure 20: A Six-Stage Planning Model

Stage 1: Prepare

The initial stage is one of preparation. Begin by forming a group to be responsible for the planning process. The group's name is not really important; it might be a planning committee, a steering committee, a study group, or even a task force. The size of the group has not really been a critical variable, either, in our experience. Our general guideline is to create a group that is large enough to represent the key decision makers or stakeholders and small enough to be able to meet and work together effectively. Consider including interested and motivated people who represent the district's central administration, building administration, teachers, parents, community leaders, and students. At least one person should bring to the group a good knowledge base, training, and, if possible, experience in contemporary approaches to gifted/talented education and the LoS approach. The goals of this stage are to gather, share, and discuss information; create a shared understanding of the rationale and goals of LoS; make an informed commitment to developing and implementing programming; and to pave the way for the development of successful programming.

Stage 2: Clarify Where You Are Now

This stage involves taking stock of your current activities, practices, and resources relating to LoS programming, carrying out a systematic assessment of needs at the district level and within each school, and examining the school's culture and climate for deliberate efforts to recognize and nurture students' strengths and talents. Your goals are to determine your current status, identify the positives that are already in place, and explore the major areas of opportunity and need for program development.

Stage 3: Deciding Where to Go Next

This stage involves setting goals at the district and school levels for implementing LoS programming. During this stage, you will explore goals and specific actions that will help you to sustain or expand the positive commitments that are already in place, as well as to set goals for attaining your "wish list" of new or improved services for students. In this stage, you will engage in strategic planning for action, making decisions about your programming needs at the district and school levels and mobilizing people and resources to enable programming to move forward.

Stage 4: Carry Out Programming

The major focus of this stage is actually implementing LoS. It is important to move to the action stage and not let planning become an endless stream of meetings and discussions! Through your efforts to put LoS into practice, you will discover what's working, what needs improvement, and emerging new opportunities and challenges to address. If you wait until you believe you have designed the elusive "perfect" model, you may never get to the point at which you actually serve your students' needs. In the LoS approach, programming—actually carrying out talent development activities with students—is the "engine that pulls the entire train."

Stage 5: Seek Talents and Strengths

Although traditional gifted programming models have emphasized identifying a specific group of gifted students who become eligible for programming, the LoS approach provides a rather different opportunity. By placing your initial emphasis on understanding and carrying out programming at the four levels, you will find new ways to search for and recognize strengths and talents among individual students. By working as "talent spotters" and by providing a variety of programming opportunities for many students (or even for all students, at Level I), you will begin to identify in a very natural and dynamic way students who will benefit from more advanced or extensive opportunities (such as Level III and IV services). You can also examine data about your students based on many sources (teacher or parent observations or recommendations, performance data, or test scores) to help you identify their talent development strengths and needs—including data about students whose strengths and talents were previously "hidden" or difficult to identify.

Stage 6: Ensure Quality, Innovation and Continuous Improvement

As you implement LoS programming, it is important to document your activities, not only to celebrate your successes, but also to identify areas that need improvement or new areas to develop. This involves continuous monitoring of progress, openness to innovation, commitment to improvement, and engaging in professional development. This stage also involves evaluating programming to promote and support effective decision making. Note that the activities in Stage 6 also provide input for on-going planning; the overall planning model proposes a continuous process of monitoring, managing, and modifying programming, rather than viewing planning as a finite "event" or activity.

Implementing LoS at the Classroom, School, or District Level

Figures 21, 22, and 23 summarize specific suggestions for implementing LoS programming effectively and efficiently at various levels. It is possible for individual teachers to implement many essential ingredients of the LoS approach in their own classroom by following the suggestions in Figure 21. The staff of a school can also make a commitment to implementing LoS on a buildingwide basis; Figure 22 presents suggestions for the schoolwide level of implementation. The most comprehensive approach to implementing LoS is on a districtwide basis, and Figure 23 summarizes our recommendations for districtwide commitments to LoS.

Implementing Levels of Service (LoS) in a Class

- *Look* every day for students' strengths and talents in many different ways. Be a "talent spotter!"

- *Talk* with students about their strengths, special interests, and talents.

- Encourage students to *explore* different areas and *look* for their own strengths.

- *Assess* students' learning styles and help them to understand the results and to know how they learn and work best.

- Construct *talent profiles* and *talent action* or *growth plans* and involve the students in the process.

- *Design* the classroom as a flexible, multitalent learning laboratory; create a *climate* conducive to creative learning and inquiry.

- Teach students how to use many kinds of *tools* to extend their own learning and productivity (e.g., technology, thinking tools, time/organization tools, product and presentation tools).

- Teach *metacognitive* and *self-direction* skills and help students use them.

- Use a variety of learning activities, including *circle of knowledge*, *team learning*, and varied "hands-on, minds-on" activities.

- Discuss and apply criteria for *quality* work and *creative* products.

- Incorporate *productive thinking* (creative thinking, critical thinking, problem solving, and decision making) into instruction for all students on a daily basis.

- Be *alert* for students with special talents and interests that relate to any topic or curricular area and for students who may need more challenge or advancement in learning activities.

- *Involve* parents and community resource people or groups in searching for talents and strengths and in learning projects.

- *Guide* all students in planning, carrying out, sharing, and evaluating learning projects and independent inquiry (individually and in small groups).

- *Link* classroom learning with out-of-school events, places, and resources.

Figure 21: Implementing LoS in a Class

Implementing Levels of Service (LoS) in a School

- Create, monitor, follow, and revise a *school action plan* with specific vision and goal statements for talent development.

- Support *learning style* and *profiling* processes schoolwide.

- Create opportunities for teachers to *exchange* and *share* ideas and resources.

- Provide *materials* and *time* for curriculum and instructional development.

- Provide support and guidance for teachers to *discuss* students' strengths and talents to work together to respond to student needs.

- Provide access to *technology* in all classrooms, not just in one lab.

- Examine *school climate* and work to sustain or enhance a healthy one.

- Create *curricular enhancement* teams to stimulate innovation.

- *Cluster* students in talent and interest areas for parts of the school day to provide services that cut across classroom or grade-level boundaries.

- Offer time and opportunities on a weekly basis (at least) for talent *exploration* and *sharing* on a cross-age basis. Involve staff and community resource people, too.

- Create and draw upon a *community resource pool*. Develop opportunities for *mentoring* and *role modeling* in talent and career areas.

- Form *partnerships* with other community agencies or organizations.

- Make your school a *lighthouse for learning*—a place where people of all ages can pursue learning in various talent areas.

- Support a variety of *optional* and *invitational* learning activities and programs (e.g., contests, quiz bowls, Odyssey of the Mind, Future Problem Solving, Young Inventors).

- Provide scheduled time and support for staff to review and discuss all students' *talent profiles* and *talent action/growth plans*.

- *Benchmark* and *celebrate* exemplary progress and products. *Display* and *promote* creative accomplishments of staff and students.

- Create a *bank* of enrichment units or learning projects for staff to exchange.

- Provide time for one or more staff to serve as LoS specialists or *catalysts*.

Figure 22: Implementing LoS in a School

Implementing Levels of Service (LoS) in a District

- Create a *district master plan* to guide policy and program development. Strive for support and commitment to sustaining programming efforts.

- Provide regular opportunities for teachers (individually, in groups or teams, and within or among schools) to *share* both successful practices and concerns.

- *Adopt* a philosophy statement consistent with the *LoS Fundamental Tenets and Belief Statements* and provide resources to support its implementation.

- Promote *community awareness* of the LoS approach and its benefits.

- Provide opportunities and support for appropriate, sustained *professional development*; move beyond one-shot or "entertainment" presentations.

- Initiate, conduct, and use the results of a systematic *evaluation* of programming.

- Encourage and support programming that *cuts across* age, grade, or building lines.

- Support initiatives that contribute to *continuous improvement* and to innovation at the classroom, school, and district levels.

- Be open to *experimentation* and share the results.

- Work together to use structured problem-solving and decision-making methods and tools to *address new opportunities, challenges,* or *concerns.*

- Promote *continuous learning* by staff, including involvement in professional literature and organizations.

- Seek *creative funding* through grants and special project funding.

Figure 23: Implementing LoS in a District

Indicators of Quality in Programming

How can you determine whether your programming efforts meet or exceed reasonable standards of quality? In areas as complex as teaching and learning and serving as diverse an array of stakeholders as schools must, it can be very difficult, indeed, to respond with confidence to this question. The search for an appropriate response that can be defended on the basis of research and theory, as well as logic and personal values, will probably begin by examining the school's results and outcomes in relation to its stated vision, mission, goals, and objectives. No universal agreement has been attained regarding how to compare or evaluate a school's selection of goals. In addition, it is often exceedingly difficult to attach specific performance standards or criteria to many of the goals we consider important, especially more complex outcomes at higher cognitive (e.g., productive thinking, creativity, and problem solving) or affective (e.g., resourcefulness, love of learning, self-management) levels. A school's on-going analysis, review, and evaluation of its efforts should always seek ways, both quantitatively and qualitatively, to document the goals it holds important, and to keep evaluation from being to the level at which the most easily measured outcomes (e.g., memorization and recall of information) become, by default, its most important outcomes.

Similarly, we recommend caution when using and interpreting standardized achievement test results, especially in relation to LoS programming outcomes. Minimum competencies are not necessarily indicators of effectiveness, even for at-risk students; schools should not permit minimum competencies to become maximum expectancies for any student. By the same token, high achievement scores are not necessarily an indication of successful instruction or appropriate challenge for students. Some students may attain high scores on the basis of what they already knew prior to instruction, rather than as a reflection of high-quality, challenging instruction. Some students who attain very high achievement scores may simply be getting by on what they already know, rather than being challenged to progress to higher or more complex levels.

We must be mindful of the warning issued by Julian Stanley that there is more variability in the 99th percentile than in the rest of the distribution. That is, when a student's score is at the 99th percentile, we only know that the test was not able to tell us about how much beyond its ceiling (if at all) a student might have been able to respond successfully. Some students might have reached their limit in the very next group of questions, if there had been another group, whereas others might have continued on successfully through many more complex and challenging levels.

Evaluating LoS Programming

How will you determine the quality, effectiveness, or impact of your programming efforts? How will you document whether you have done what you intended and planned to do and what the results or outcomes of those efforts have been? What components or aspects of your LoS programming and school improvement efforts have been most and least successful? What should be done to sustain exemplary practices or to modify and improve practices that have not been successful?

Evaluation should provide information that will help you to assess the strengths and weaknesses of any programming effort and to make judgments about program quality and support. In addition, evaluation should guide future planning. It is important to consider the degree to which innovation is encouraged and supported within the schools—how existing efforts can be improved and how new efforts will be initiated.

Evaluation of LoS programming is a difficult but important consideration for all districts and schools. Evaluating programming may be difficult for several reasons, including:

1. Complex outcomes, such as those commonly stated for LoS programming, are not easy to measure.

2. The full impact or benefits of programming for students may not be evident immediately.

3. The more effectively you integrate various components of your school program, the more difficult it becomes to isolate the impact of any of those components.

4. The greater the variety of services offered, the more diverse the criteria needed to assess their effectiveness.

Evaluation is not a one-shot, one-time event. Thorough, effective, useful evaluation should be a continuous process of identifying ways to strengthen or improve your efforts. Evaluation should be a natural process that enables programs to be modified and made more effective. In programming for talent development through LoS, a sense of incompleteness is healthy—recognizing that accomplishing one's goals and attaining excellence in one area of programming is an on-going process.

There are many models or approaches to program evaluation. In general, however, we believe there is substantial agreement that effective evaluation involves:

- **Advance Planning.** Plans for evaluation should be made as part of the initial planning process, not after program implementation has already begun. A common error, for example, is to defer consideration of evaluation until it is too late to gather appropriate pretest or "baseline" data upon which later assessments of change or growth may depend.

- **Agreement on the Purposes to Be Served.** The purposes and need for evaluation of programming efforts should be clearly understood by everyone involved before the evaluation process begins.

- **Recognition of the Varying Needs of Different "Stakeholders."** While there may be many questions of common interest or concern to all who will be involved in the evaluation process, certain objectives of the evaluation, and the kinds of data needed to assess them, may vary or be quite unique from one target audience to another. That is, the questions and concerns of parents, administrators, board members, and staff members may differ and may also involve different kinds of evidence or documentation. These differences should be taken into account when planning the evaluation.

- **Clear Goals and Well-Defined Objectives.** In order to facilitate effective and useful evaluation, the goals and objectives for programming should be stated in terms that make clear the kinds of data (or evidence) that will permit them to be assessed.

- **Specific Recommendations.** The evaluation effort should result in specific recommendations regarding modifications or revisions of support, action, or content of programming that will enhance program effectiveness. Good evaluation efforts lead to improvement planning and decision making.

- **Both Qualitative and Quantitative Data Are Valuable.** Evaluation of the complex outcomes that are typical of programming cannot be accomplished solely by the use of standardized achievement tests or other strictly quantitative data and test scores. Effective evaluation documents the real activities and accomplishments of students. Test data may be one valuable component of program evaluation, but they are not likely to be the only data. And, in many cases, they might not even be the primary data for evaluation. For example, a 15% increase in students' fluency scores may be impressive to some people, while actual evidence of students' applications, such as solving problems at home or in school, may be much more important and impressive to many others.

- **An Outside Evaluator, Whenever Possible.** Although there may be less consensus in the field of educational evaluation regarding this subject, many specialists agree that an outside evaluator, who will be more likely to be objective and impartial than an in-house evaluator, can offer important insights and recommendations.

- **Authentic Tasks and Authentic Assessment.** As we begin to focus more and more on creating tasks or learning experiences that relate instructional content to the ways it will be used or applied in real-world contexts (authentic tasks), we also face the need for new ways of assessing students' attainment of those outcomes. As a result, there has also been growing interest in authentic assessment, including nontest demonstrations of performance by individuals or groups on real or realistic tasks, open-ended project evaluation, and documentation of student outcomes using a portfolio approach.

Innovation and Change

Effective evaluation can also provide directions and challenge for innovation and change, identifying significant areas of need or opportunity for new activities or services. In order to be effective in managing change, educators, administrators, and policymakers in today's schools must be prepared to gather data from many sources and use those data to monitor and revise their present policies and actions. It is no longer possible in today's world to assume that curricular, instructional methods and resources, or the characteristics, needs, and interests of students will remain static for long periods of time. Effective schools are those in which people work to establish and maintain relatively short cycles of response to change (that is, create and apply flexible, responsive modes of action to effect change without long delays for review, analysis and reanalysis, and approval).

Continuous Improvement

Obviously, no programming efforts are ever perfect; there is always room for improvement. It is important to accept the challenge to be constantly alert to new ways to improve and do things better—your goal, and your standard operating procedure, will focus on continuous improvement, rather than on "just good enough." The better you become at defining the outcomes you consider essential for every student, the better you will be able to determine whether or not you have been successful. You must always be examining your policies, practices, and results in order to be alert for better ways to recognize and develop students' strengths, talents, and sustained interests and to ensure their competence, confidence, and commitment as learners.

Continuous improvement is not only a matter of finding things that are insufficient, wrong, inadequate, or deficient; it is not just fixing up something that is damaged or not working right. It will be just as important—and undoubtedly much more satisfying and renewing—to keep in mind that every good school always seeks ways to become better. Thus, as some important goals are attained, new ones emerge. As innovation occurs within a school, a climate is established in which more new ideas can be encouraged in the future. Growth must be planned and well managed in order to avoid a helter-skelter approach in which nothing seems stable for very long. But, at the same time, it is also necessary to avoid the dangers of complacency, failure to examine carefully the strengths and weaknesses of the program over time, or rigidity in the face of changing circumstances and needs.

Continuing Evaluation and Long-Range Planning

Evaluating and documenting your programming efforts and results also involve careful continuing evaluation, long-range planning, and revision of programming policies and practices.

Designing regular updates or revisions. Effective programming is dynamic, not static, and talent development is a new and rapidly changing area in which new developments in theory and research occur frequently. On the plus side, this stimulates many opportunities for school improvement and program refinement; the minus side, of course, is that it can be difficult to keep up to date without on-going effort and study. For this reason, you must recognize that policies and procedures for LoS programming must be reviewed regularly. All plans should be viewed as flexible and open to continuous efforts at improvement, rather than as fixed and permanent in the form in which they were originally created. This calls for on-going investigation of new trends and direction in the field, discussion of many alternatives for program growth, and time and effort devoted to long-range planning and the establishment of both districtwide and building-level priorities and goals.

Long-range planning. The challenges of change and continuous improvement suggest that the planning committees should give serious consideration to planning over a 3–5 year period. These efforts should be on-going, so that planning will be deliberate and systematic, rather than haphazard. When program development or change represents a hurried set of decisions made under the pressure of crises (real or imaginary), the results are not likely to be satisfactory to anyone for very long.

Communication and School–Community Relations

Finally, documentation of your programming involves efforts to inform, educate, and communicate with the public and to disseminate the accomplishments and successes of your programming efforts.

Answering questions. There will always be many, varied, and unusual questions from community members and parents, as well as from staff members who were not directly involved in the initial program planning efforts. There will be some, for example, who will want to know more about district or school policies and procedures in general or compare them with other programs they may have heard or read about elsewhere. These questions may arise from a general curiosity or interest, from concerns for proceeding in the best possible manner, or by virtue of people's concern for and interest in their own children's educational services or programs.

Such questions are important and valid and deserve honest and informed responses. When there are concerns about one district's policies and procedures compared to what they have heard from other places, or when there are discussions of differences in specific activities from one school to another within a district, it is important that the staff members have a common base of information to work with and that staff and administrators know how to get information to prevent incorrect information from being given out inadvertently.

Disseminate program accomplishments and promote good public relations. All schools should be alert to any opportunities to document their accomplishments and success for members of their community and to promote positive, cooperative relations within the community. Community members often read, hear, or see only a small sample of the school's activities and accomplishments (e.g., the attainments of winning athletic teams or an annual school dramatic performance, or perhaps the honor roll or features about scholarship or award winners). Too often, the publicity is neutral, controversial, or even negative—such as budget, construction, or contract issues; publication of achievement test scores and comparisons among districts (whether or not appropriate); Board election campaigns; or special issues that arise. You can seek opportunities to promote activities and accomplishments throughout the year to build awareness of your efforts to recognize and develop the talents and strengths of many students.

There is some disagreement in the literature on the issue of how *visible* LoS programming should be or in what ways. Those who argue for a high level of visibility for talent development programs feel that visibility is essential to maintaining support for funding and staff. Others believe that the accomplishments of many staff and students can be promoted with less-explicit emphasis in the publicity on "the gifted teachers" or "the gifted students." They believe that the important focus should be on the *activities and accomplishments themselves, not on labels for the participants.* When the time comes for the district's LoS programming (and budget) to be reviewed, policymakers can be informed that the existence of LoS programming in the district enabled those accomplishments to happen. (If this goes unnoticed, you will certainly be able to offer a reminder.) When many staff and community members have shared in the activities and the publicity, programming is more likely to gain support; traditional arguments for support for programs often appear to be special-purpose requests lacking a broad base of support. Regardless of one's viewpoint on "visibility," there is broad agreement that publicity and good public relations efforts are important for successful programming and must be conducted deliberately, not left to chance.

The Rest of the Story ...

The Lakeside schools' commitment to, and investments in, planning, documentation, and evaluation contributed substantially to the success of their programming. The district's involvement of many stakeholders (including administrators, faculty, parents, and community members) led to a program that was effectively woven into the fabric of education in the community. Their sustained work contributed significantly, for example, to protecting and sustaining their programming and personnel during a time of financial stress on school budgets in their community—when several other neighboring areas were reducing or eliminating their gifted programs.

As a result of the overall program evaluation, the district was able to identify many positive outcomes and benefits of LoS programming. The evaluation report provided evidence to help school leaders answer questions from staff and parents and to identify several areas that needed improvement.

The LoS programming specialists in the Lakeside community schools decided that it was important, for them personally and for the district, to document carefully their time and activities with students, teachers, and outside resource people and groups, as well as their activities during their weekly team meetings. The specialists found that there were many challenging and rewarding dimensions to their roles, but that they were also called upon to be advocates, diplomats, public relations persons, and problem solvers in a variety of different situations. Their role was dynamic and evolving and, in many ways, quite different from their previous experience as classroom teachers. They found that there were different levels of understanding and support among parents, administrators, and classroom teachers in each of the schools throughout the district. They also discovered that they needed to have and use good time management skills, conferencing, and interpersonal relations skills. They discovered that a major task in dealing with parents involved concerns that students' needs might not be met because the district did not have the same kind of highly visible pull-out program that was offered in neighboring districts. The district's support for LoS programming included providing a number of professional development opportunities to assist the specialists in addressing their challenges.

One of the most significant results of the specialists' careful documentation of their work and the program evaluation was to propose to the school board (and to accomplish, with the board's support) an expansion of the specialist staff, so that each school would have its own full-time

LoS specialist. The district's investment in planning, professional development, awareness and information for many stakeholders, and thorough evaluation contributed significantly to the district's success in programming.

The Lakeside LoS programming continued to grow, and, over several years of work, it became integrated into the district's overall approach to educating and nurturing all students. The district's administration and staff, along with parents and community leaders, recognized that talent development was everybody's business. In the beginning of this book, we proposed that programming includes "all of the efforts made—at home, in a classroom, the district, and the community—to recognize, nurture, and celebrate the many and varied strengths, talents, and sustained interests of all students." We believe that it is possible for any school or school district, through planning, training, deliberate action, and sustained effort, to translate that vision into effective practice.

Appendix
Recommended Readings and Resources

Books and Articles

Amabile, T. (1992). *Growing up creative.* Buffalo, NY: Creative Education Foundation.

Baum, S., Gable, R., & List, K. (1998). *Chi square, Pie charts, and me.* Mansfield Center, CT: Creative Learning Press.

Clark, G. A., & Zimmerman, E. (1986). *Educating artistically talented students.* Syracuse, NY: Syracuse University Press.

Clark, G. A., & Zimmerman, E. (1994). *Programming opportunities for students gifted and talented in the visual arts* (RBDM series, 9402). Storrs: National Research Center on the Gifted and Talented, University of Connecticut.

Dunn, R., & Dunn, K. (1978). *Teaching students through their individual learning styles.* Reston, VA: Reston Publishing.

Dunn, R., Dunn, K., & Treffinger, D. J. (1992). *Bringing out the giftedness in your child.* New York: Wiley.

Gregory, G. H., & Chapman, C. (2002). *Differentiating instruction: One size doesn't fit all.* New York: Corwin.

Haroutounian, J. (2002). *Kindling the spark: Recognizing and developing musical talent.* New York: Oxford University Press.

Heacox, D. (2001). *Differentiating instruction in the regular classroom: How to reach and teach all learners grades 3–12.* Minneapolis, MN: Free Spirit.

Isaksen, S. G., Dorval, K. B., & Treffinger, D. J. (1998). *Toolbox for creative problem solving: Basic tools and resources.* Williamsville, NY: Creative Problem Solving Group.

Isaksen, S. G., Dorval, K. B., & Treffinger, D. J. (2000). *Creative approaches to problem solving* (2nd ed.). Dubuque, IA: Kendall/Hunt.

Johnsen, S., & Johnson, K. (1996). *Independent study program.* Waco, TX: Prufrock Press.

Karnes, F. A., & Chauvin, J. C. (1999). *Leadership development program.* Scottsdale, AZ: Great Potential Press.

Keller-Mathers, S., & Puccio, K. (2000). *Big tools for young thinkers.* Waco, TX: Prufrock Press.

Landrum, M., Callahan, C., & Shaklee, B. (2001). *Aiming for excellence: Annotations to the NAGC pre-K–grade 12 gifted program standards.* Waco, TX: Prufrock Press.

Lawrence, G. (1993). *People types and tiger stripes* (3rd ed.). Gainesville, FL: Center for Applications of Psychological Type.

McCluskey, K., & Treffinger, D. J. (2002). *Enriching teaching and learning for talent development.* Sarasota, FL: Center for Creative Learning.

Nash, D. (2001, December). Enter the mentor. *Parenting for High Potential,* 18–21.

Nash. D., & Treffinger, D. J. (1993). *The mentor kit.* Waco, TX: Prufrock Press.

National Association for Gifted Children (2000). *Pre-K–grade 12 gifted program standards.* Washington, DC: Author. (Available online at www.nagc.org)

Noller, R. B. (1997). *Mentoring: A voiced scarf.* Sarasota, FL: Center for Creative Learning.

Parks, S., & Black, H. (1997). *Building thinking skills.* Pacific Grove, CA: Critical Thinking Books and Software.

Puccio, K., Keller-Mathers, S., & Treffinger, D. J. (2000). *Adventures in real problem solving.* Waco, TX: Prufrock Press.

Purcell, J., Renzulli, J., McCoach, B., & Spottiswoode, H. (2001, December). The magic of mentorships. *Parenting for High Potential,* 22–26.

Reilly, J. (1992). *Mentorship.* Scottsdale, AZ: Great Potential Press.

Renzulli, J., Gentry, M., & Reis, S. (2003). *Enrichment clusters: A practical plan for real-world, student-driven learning.* Mansfield Center, CT: Creative Learning Press.

Roberts, J., & Inman, T. (2001, December). Mentoring and your child: Developing a successful relationship. *Parenting for High Potential,* 8–10.

Schlichter, C. L., & Palmer, R. (1993). *Thinking smart: A primer of the talents unlimited model.* Mansfield Center, CT: Creative Learning Press.

Selby, E. C., & Young, G. C. (2001, September). A harvest of talent. *Parenting for High Potential,* 8–11,25.

Selby, E. C., Treffinger, D. J., & Isaksen, S. G. (2002). *VIEW: An assessment of problem solving style.* Sarasota, FL: Center for Creative Learning.

Starko, A. (1986). *It's about time.* Mansfield Center, CT: Creative Learning Press.

Starko, A. J. (2000). *Creativity in the classroom: Schools of curious delight* (2nd ed.). Mahwah, NJ: Erlbaum.

Starko, A. J., & Schack, G. D. (1992). *Looking for data in all the right places.* Mansfield Center, CT: Creative Learning Press.

Starko, A. J., & Schack, G. D. (1998). *Research comes alive!* Mansfield Center, CT: Creative Learning Press.

Tomlinson, C. (1999). *The differentiated classroom: Responding to the needs of all learners.* Alexandria, VA: Association for Supervision and Curriculum Development.

Tomlinson, C. (2001). *How to differentiate instruction in mixed ability classrooms.* Alexandria, VA: Association for Supervision and Curriculum Development.

Tomlinson, C., & Allan, S. (2000). *Leadership for differentiated schools and classrooms.* Alexandria, VA: Association for Supervision and Curriculum Development.

Tomlinson, C., Kaplan, S., Renzulli, J., Purcell, J., Leppien, J., & Burns, D. (2002). *The parallel curriculum.* New York: Corwin Press.

Torrance, E. P. (1995). *Why Fly? A philosophy of creativity.* Norwood, NJ: Ablex.

Treffinger, D. J. (2000a). *Creative problem solver's guidebook.* Waco, TX: Prufrock Press.

Treffinger, D. J. (2000b). *Practice problems for CPS.* Waco, TX: Prufrock Press.

Treffinger, D. J., & Feldhusen, J. F. (1998). *Planning for productive thinking and learning.* Sarasota, FL: Center for Creative Learning.

Treffinger, D. J., Isaksen, S. G., & Dorval, K. B. (2000). *Creative problem solving: An introduction* (3rd. ed.). Waco, TX: Prufrock Press.

Treffinger, D. J., & Nassab, C. A. (2000). *Thinking tools lessons.* Waco, TX: Prufrock Press.

Treffinger, D. J., Nassab, C. A., Schoonover, P. F., Selby, E. C., Shepardson, C. A., Wittig, C. V., & Young, G. C. (2004). *The CPS kit.* Waco, TX: Prufrock Press.

Treffinger, D. J., Nassab, C. A., Schoonover, P. F., Selby, E. C., Shepardson, C. A., Wittig, C. V., & Young, G. C. (2003a). *Thinking with standards—preparing for the future (elementary).* Waco, TX: Prufrock Press.

Treffinger, D. J., Nassab, C. A., Schoonover, P. F., Selby, E. C., Shepardson, C. A., Wittig, C. V., & Young, G. C. (2003b). *Thinking with standards—Preparing for the future (middle).* Waco, TX: Prufrock Press.

Treffinger, D. J., Nassab, C. A., Schoonover, P. F., Selby, E. C., Shepardson, C. A., Wittig, C. V., & Young, G. C. (2003c). *Thinking with standards—preparing for the future (secondary).* Waco, TX: Prufrock Press.

Treffinger, D. J., & Young, G. C. (2002). *Building creative excellence.* Glassboro, NJ: Destination ImagiNation.

Treffinger, D. J., Young, G. C., Selby, E. C., & Shepardson, C. A. (2002). *Assessing creativity: A guide for educators.* Storrs: National Research Center on the Gifted and Talented, University of Connecticut.

Winebrenner, S. (2000). *Teaching gifted kids in the regular classroom.* Minneapolis, MN: Free Spirit.

Young, G. C., & Selby, G. C. (2001, September). Recognizing and developing talent: Key elements of the journey for youth orchestra members. *Parenting for High Potential,* 18–24.

Organizations and Programs

1. **Camp Invention®**, a program of the National Inventor's Hall of Fame, is a one-week day camp for children entering grades 2–6. The program is hosted by schools throughout the country each summer. Camp Invention® provides children with the opportunity to create new possibilities and discover solutions through hands-on learning. The program involves teamwork, creative problem solving, and inventive thinking.
Camp Invention
221 S. Broadway
Akron, OH 44308
(330) 849-8528
http://www.invent.org

2. The **Center for Creative Learning** offers a variety of resources, instruments, and services to support planning, professional development, implementation, and evaluation of the LoS approach. In addition to its focus on LoS programming for talent development, the Center's work deals with creative learning, Creative Problem Solving (CPS), and problem-solving style (with emphasis on the VIEW style assessment). The Center's Web site includes a variety of downloadable resources.
Center for Creative Learning
P.O. Box 14100–NE Plaza
Sarasota, FL 34278-4100
(941) 342-9928
http://www.creativelearning.com

3. The **College Board's Advanced Placement Program** is a cooperative educational endeavor between secondary schools and colleges and universities. Since its inception in 1955, the program has provided motivated high school students with the opportunity to take college-level courses in a high school setting and, in many cases, to earn college credit while they are still in high school. The program offers 35 courses in 19 subject areas.
The College Board—AP Program
45 Columbus Ave.
New York, NY 10023
(212) 713-8000
http://apcentral.collegeboard.com

4. The **Craftsman/NSTA Young Inventors Award Program** challenges students in grades 2–8 to use creativity and imagination along with science, technology, and mechanical ability to invent or modify a tool. This competition began in 1996. Students must work independently to conceive and

design their tool inventions. The student, with guidance from a teacher-advisor, parent, or significant adult, designs and builds a tool. The tool must perform a practical function, including (but not limited to) tools that mend, make life easier or safer in some way, entertain, or solve an everyday problem.

National Science Teachers Association (NSTA)
1840 Wilson Blvd.
Arlington, VA 22201
(888) 494-4994
http://www.nsta.org/programs/craftsman

5. **Destination ImagiNation, Inc.,** seeks to help young people discover, develop, and apply creativity and creative problem solving. The program has two major components: Team Challenges and Instant Challenges. Instant Challenges present students with challenges that require them to use their imagination to respond quickly and decisively. Team Challenges engage the students in working collaboratively and cooperatively to deal with one of the five yearlong challenges. The teams conduct research and use their creative and critical thinking skills to devise original solutions and performances. Teams throughout the world can engage in local, regional, state, and a global finals tournament. The program serves more than 100,000 students from the elementary through the university years in 47 states, three Canadian provinces, and 14 countries outside North America.

Destination ImagiNation®
P.O. Box 547
Glassboro, NJ 08028
(856) 881-1603
http://www.destinationimagination.org

6. The **FIRST LEGO League** is often described as the "Little League" of the FIRST Robotics Competition. (FIRST is an acronym representing "For Inspiration and Recognition of Science and Technology.") The LEGO League program is the result of a partnership between FIRST and the LEGO Company, that seeks to inspire and celebrate science and technology for children ages 9 through 14 using real-world context and hands-on experimentation.

FIRST LEGO League
US First
200 Bedford St.
Manchester, NH 03101
(800) 871-8326
http://www.usfirst.org

7. The **Future Problem Solving Program (FPSP)** engages students in creative problem solving. The program stimulates critical and creative thinking skills and encourages students to develop a vision for the future. FPSP features curricular and cocurricular competitive, as well as noncompetitive, activities in creative problem solving and serves students at the elementary, middle, and high school levels. The Community Problem Solving Program (CmPS) involves students in identifying and solving significant problems and challenges in their own community.
Future Problem Solving Program
2028 Regency Rd.
Lexington, KY 40503
(800) 256-1499
http://www.fpsp.org

8. The **Great Books Foundation** is dedicated to helping people of all ages learn how to think and share ideas by educating them to become participants in, leaders of, and advocates for shared inquiry. Through text-based discussion of outstanding works of literature, shared inquiry strengthens critical thinking and civil discourse, promotes reading and the appreciation of literature, and provides people of all ages with a powerful instrument for social engagement and lifelong learning.
Great Books Foundation
35 East Wacker Dr., Ste. 2300
Chicago, IL 60601-2298
(800) 222-5870
http://www.greatbooks.org

9. The **Intel Science Talent Search (STS)** is a long-established and highly regarded precollege science competition. For more than 60 years, this competition has provided an incentive and an arena for U.S. high school seniors to complete an original research project and have it recognized by a national jury of highly regarded professional scientists. The projects are a result of inquiry-based learning methods designed to nurture critical reasoning skills, to experience science through the use of the scientific method, and to demonstrate how math and science skills are crucial to making sense of today's technological world and making the best decisions for tomorrow.
Intel Science Talent Search
Science Service
1719 N St., NW
Washington, DC 20036
(202) 785-2255
http://www.sciserv.org/sts/
or http://www.intel.com/education/sts/

10. Recognizing and responding to students' individual learning styles are important elements of any effort to implement the LoS approach. For more information about learning styles, with an emphasis on the Dunn and Dunn model, contact the **International Learning Styles Network.**
International Learning Styles Network
St. John's University
8000 Utopia Parkway
Jamaica, NY 11439
http://www.learningstyles.net

11. The **International Telementoring Program** is a virtual mentoring program for upper elementary or older students. Telementoring is an electronic version of the age-old practice in which an older, more experienced person shares his or her experiences and expertise with a younger "protégé." Through the relationship, the student protégé gains insights about the real world, explores new ideas, and is inspired to pursue special interests.
Keystone Science School
3919 Benthaven Dr.
Fort Collins, CO 80526
(970) 206-9352
http://www.telementor.org

12. **INVENT AMERICA!** is a nonprofit K–8 education program launched in 1987 that helps children develop creative thinking and problem-solving skills through a fun, unique and proven learning tool—inventing! INVENT AMERICA! gives teachers tools to help them encourage productive thinking skills in students.
Invent America
P.O. Box 26065
Alexandria, VA 22313
http://www.inventamerica.com

13. **Math Olympiads for Elementary and Middle Schools** (grades 4–6 or 7–8) seeks to stimulate enthusiasm and a love for mathematics. Students in a school's math club meet weekly for an hour. The club members explore a topic or strategy in depth or they practice for the contests using nonroutine problems. The highlights for students are the five monthly contests given from November to March. No traveling is required. These contests provide an incentive for students to intensify their study of math.
Math Olympiads
2154 Bellmore Ave.
Bellmore, NY 11710
http://www.moems.org

14. Two major organizations that provide programs and resources relating to musical talent and its development are the **American Symphony Orchestra League** (http://www.symphony.org) and **Bands of America** (http://www.bands.org). The MusicLink foundation (http://www.musiclinkfoundation.org) is a nonprofit organization that provides opportunities for promising musical students to develop their talent through its LessonLink and StudyLink programs.

15. The **National Association for Gifted Children (NAGC)** is a nonprofit organization of parents, teachers, educators, community leaders, and other professionals who unite to address the unique needs of all children and youth with demonstrated gifts and talents, as well as those who may be able to develop their talent potential with appropriate educational experiences. NAGC's publications include *Gifted Child Quarterly* and *Parenting for High Potential.*
National Association for Gifted Children
1707 L St., NW, Ste. 550
Washington, DC 20036
(202) 785-4268.
http://www.nagc.org

16. Each year, thousands of schools in the United States participate in the **National Geographic Bee** using materials prepared by the National Geographic Society. The contest is designed to encourage teachers to include geography in their classrooms, spark student interest in the subject, and increase public awareness about geography. Schools with students in grades 4–8 are eligible for this entertaining and challenging test of geographic knowledge.
National Geographic Society
P.O. Box 98199
Washington, D.C. 20090-8199
(800) 647-5463
http://www.nationalgeographic.com/geographybee

17. Through the **National PTA Reflections Program**, students in preschool through grade 12 are encouraged to create and submit works of art in four areas: literature, musical composition, photography, and the visual arts. Students participate in the Reflections Program by submitting entries to their local PTA or PTSA. Entries may be created as a classroom assignment or independently at home. National PTA's Reflections Program is designed to enhance, rather than replace, a quality arts education. It provides opportunities for students to express themselves and to receive positive recognition for their artistic efforts.
National PTA
330 N. Wabash Ave.
Ste. 2100

Chicago, IL 60611
(800) 307-4782
http://www.pta.org/parentinvolvement/familyfun/aboutreflect.asp

18. The **National Research Center on the Gifted and Talented (NRC-G/T)** is a federally supported center specifically committed to conducting and disseminating research on important topics in gifted education. NRC-G/T offers a variety of research-based resources to support contemporary approaches to talent development.
NRC-G/T
University of Connecticut, Neag School of Education
2131 Hillside Rd., Unit 3007
Storrs, CT 06269-3007
(860) 486-4676
http://www.gifted.uconn.edu/nrcgt.html

19. **People to People Student Ambassadors** travel overseas for 2–3 weeks during the summer to learn, share, and represent their communities and schools. The program encourages meaningful exchanges between young people of different cultures through official meetings, educational site visits, and home stays, all of which create deep cultural understanding, probe a nation's history, and launch long-lasting friendships. By becoming a Student Ambassador, participants in grades 6–12 gain an appreciation for the world in which they live, build their self-confidence, enrich their education through learning in the global classroom, and develop increased levels of maturity and independence. Experienced educators lead Student Ambassador delegations of 30–40 students.
People to People Student Ambassador Program
Dwight D. Eisenhower Bldg.
110 S. Ferrall St.
Spokane, WA 99202-4800
(509) 534-0430
http://www.studentambassadors.org

20. The **Science Olympiad** is an international nonprofit organization devoted to improving the quality of science education, increasing student interest in science, and providing recognition for outstanding achievement in science education by both students and teachers. These goals are accomplished through classroom activities, research, training workshops and the encouragement of intramural, district, regional, state and national tournaments. The Science Olympiad tournaments are rigorous academic interscholastic competitions that consist of a series of individual and team events that students prepare for during the year. The competitions follow the format of popular board games, TV shows, and athletic games. These challenging and

motivational events are well balanced between the various science disciplines of biology, earth science, chemistry, physics, computers, and technology. There is also a balance between events requiring knowledge of science facts, concepts, processes, skills, and science applications.
Science Olympiad
5955 Little Pine Lane
Rochester, MI 48306
(248) 651-4013
http://www.soinc.org

21. The purpose of the **Scripps Howard National Spelling Bee** is to help students improve their spelling, increase their vocabularies, learn concepts, and develop correct English usage that will help them all their lives. Each sponsor newspaper organizes a spelling bee program in its community, usually with the cooperation of area school officials. The champion of the sponsor's final spelling bee advances to the finals in Washington, DC. In general, the program is open to students who have not reached their 16th birthday on or before the date of the national finals and who have not passed beyond the eighth grade at the time of their school finals.
Scripps Howard National Spelling Bee
312 Walnut St., 28th Fl.
Cincinnati, OH 45202
http://www.spellingbee.com

22. **Talents Unlimited** is a teaching-learning model that integrates creative and critical thinking skills into the curriculum in any classroom arena. It is based on the Multiple Talents Approach to Learning developed by Dr. Calvin Taylor at the University of Utah. The program strives to increase student performance in specific TALENTS processes, including productive thinking, communication, forecasting, decision making, and planning with the academic talent.
Talents Unlimited
109 S. Cedar St.
Mobile, AL 36602
(334) 433-8364

23. **YouthFriends** is a program that connects caring adult volunteers with young people in schools to encourage success, promote healthy behaviors, and build stronger communities. Through YouthFriends, volunteers are linked with students ages 5–18 with shared interests like a special hobby, music, sports, reading or computers.
Youth Friends
1000 Broadway, Ste. 302
Kansas City, MO 64105

(816) 842-7082
http://www.youthfriends.org

Talent Search Programs

The **Duke University Talent Identification Program (Duke TIP)** identifies gifted children and provides resources to nurture the development of these exceptionally bright youngsters. Duke TIP provides students with the opportunity to learn more about their abilities. In fourth and fifth grade, qualifying students may participate in Duke TIP's 4th/5th Grade Talent Search (formerly MAP) program and may take advantage of its optional above-level testing. Through Duke TIP's 7th Grade Talent Search program, which focuses on the identification, recognition, and support of high-ability seventh graders, students take college entrance exams alongside high school students.

> Duke University Talent Identification Programs
> Box 90747
> Durham, NC 27708
> (919) 684-3847
> http://www.tip.duke.edu

The Johns Hopkins **Center for Talented Youth (CTY)** serves 19 U.S. states and 70 other countries. CTY's Talent Search helps families learn more about their child's math and verbal abilities. Through the Talent Search, qualifying second through eighth graders take special tests, get recognition for their abilities, perhaps qualify for special academic programs, and become part of a worldwide community of advanced learners.

> The Johns Hopkins University Center for Talented Youth (CTY)
> 3400 N. Charles St.
> Baltimore, MD 21218
> (410) 516-0337
> http://www.jhu.edu/~gifted

The **Midwest Talent Search (MTS)** and the **Midwest Talent Search for Young Students (MTSY)** are based on the premise that early and accurate assessment of students showing evidence of advanced academic abilities or achievement through out-of-level testing can be useful in designing and obtaining more appropriate academic programs for them. MTS seeks to give sixth-, seventh-, and eighth-grade students (ninth-grade ACT test takers) a more accurate picture of their mathematical and verbal reasoning abilities. Armed with this information, students and parents can reap the benefits of specialized curricula, enrichment programs, and even accelerated courses of study. MTSY seeks to give third- (scoring in the 97% or higher on a nationally normed standardized achievement test), fourth-, fifth-, and sixth-grade students (scoring in the 95% or above on a nationally normed standardized achievement test) a more accurate picture of their mathematical and verbal reasoning abilities.

Northwestern University Center for Talent Development
617 Dartmouth Place
Evanston, IL 60208
(847) 491-3782
http://www.ctdnet.acns.nwu.edu

The **Rocky Mountain Talent Search (RMTS)** is an academic talent search program providing opportunities for assessment, recognition, and special summer programs for academically talented youth. It invites capable and motivated sixth through ninth-grade students to take the SAT or ACT college entrance test not usually taken until high school. Younger students (fifth and sixth graders) take the challenging PLUS Academic Abilities Assessment. Taking these tests provides students with early experience in taking college entrance-type tests. Students who have participated over the years report increased comfort with standardized testing and significant score gains based upon Talent Search experiences.

Rocky Mountain Talent Search
Denver University Academic Youth Programs
1981 S. University Blvd.
Denver, CO 80208
(303) 871-3408
http://www.du.edu/education/ces/rmts.html